4.2   The same amount of energy is needed to accelerate the car with both engines. The energy transferred by the old engine:
$P = E \div t$, so $E = P \times t = 32\,000 \times 9.0$ *[1 mark]*
          $= 288\,000$ J *[1 mark]*
The time taken for the new engine to transfer the same amount of energy is:
$P = E \div t$, so $t = E \div P = 288\,000 \div 62\,000$ *[1 mark]*
          $= 4.645... = $ **4.6 s (to 2 s.f.)** *[1 mark]*

Page 6 — Conduction and Convection

1   Convection occurs in **liquids** and **gases**. It is where a change in **density** causes particles to move from **hotter** to **cooler** regions.
[3 marks for all correct, otherwise 2 marks for 3-4 correct, 1 mark for 1-2 correct]

2.1   E.g. make sure all of the blocks are the same thickness / make sure the blocks are identical shapes/sizes / measure the time taken for a larger change in temperature / take repeat measurements to calculate an average *[1 mark]*

2.2   Energy is transferred by heating to the kinetic energy stores of the particles at the bottom of the block *[1 mark]*. These particles collide with other particles in the block, and transfer energy mechanically to the kinetic energy stores of other particles *[1 mark]*. This continues, transferring energy through the whole block *[1 mark]*.

2.3   It has a higher thermal conductivity than the other blocks *[1 mark]*.

Pages 7-8 — Reducing Unwanted Energy Transfers

Warm-up
Wearing a more streamlined helmet

1   Thicker walls decrease the rate of energy lost from a house. Bricks with a higher thermal conductivity transfer energy at a faster rate.
[1 mark for both correct, no marks if more than two boxes have been ticked]

2.1   through the roof *[1 mark]*

2.2   E.g. install loft insulation (to reduce convection) *[1 mark]*

2.3   E.g. use draught excluders (to reduce convection) / install double glazing (to reduce conduction) / hang thick curtains (to reduce convection) / reduce the temperature difference between inside and outside the home *[1 mark for each sensible suggestion]*

3   Doing work against friction causes energy to be dissipated/ wasted (usually to thermal energy stores) *[1 mark]*. After lubricating the axle, the frictional forces acting on it were reduced *[1 mark]*. This means that less energy is dissipated as the handle (and axle) is turned and so more energy is transferred to the kinetic energy store of the handle (and axle) and the bucket *[1 mark]*.

4   Best: C   Second best: B   Worst: A *[1 mark]*
The thicker a sample is, the slower the rate of energy transfer through it *[1 mark]* so sample B will be a better insulator than sample A *[1 mark]*. Air has a lower thermal conductivity than glass (so it transfers energy at a slower rate than glass does) *[1 mark]* so even though samples B and C are the same thickness, sample C is a better insulator than sample B *[1 mark]*.

Page 9 — Efficiency

1.1   Efficiency = Useful output energy transfer
                ÷ Total input energy transfer *[1 mark]*

1.2   Efficiency = $16\,000 \div 20\,000$ *[1 mark]* = **0.8** *[1 mark]*
You'd also get the mark for giving the efficiency as a percentage (80%).

2   Efficiency = $75\% = 0.75$
Efficiency = Useful power output ÷ Total power input
So Total power input = Useful power output ÷ Efficiency
          [1 mark]
          $= 57 \div 0.75$ *[1 mark]* = **76 W** *[1 mark]*

3.1   Useful output power of the air blower:
Efficiency = Useful power output ÷ Total power input
so Useful power output = Efficiency × Total power input
          $= 0.62 \times 533$ *[1 mark]*
          $= 330.46$ W *[1 mark]*

Useful power ou
Efficiency = 13⁹
Total power inp
Useful power ou
          /

3.2   E.g. adding mor
air to hit) / incre
surface area for ι
parts of the turbine (to reduce friction) / changing the angle of the sails so they get hit by more wind *[2 marks — 1 mark for each sensible suggestion]*

Pages 10-11 — Energy Resources and Their Uses

Warm-up
Renewable — bio-fuel, solar, tidal, geothermal, wave power, hydroelectricity, wind
Non-renewable — oil, coal, gas, nuclear fuel

1   E.g. a non-renewable energy resource will one day run out *[1 mark]* but a renewable energy resource can be replenished as it is used *[1 mark]*

2.1   coal, oil, (natural) gas *[1 mark]*

2.2   E.g. generating electricity / burning coal on fires / using gas central heating / using a gas fire / coal in steam trains *[2 marks — 1 for each correct answer]*

2.3   Bio-fuels are solids, liquids or gases that are produced from plant products or from animal waste *[1 mark]*.

2.4   E.g. because fossil fuels will eventually run out / because fossil fuels harm the environment *[1 mark for any correct answer]*.

3   E.g. during winter, there are fewer hours of daylight, but the weather is usually more windy *[1 mark]*, so wind turbines will be able to generate more electricity during winter *[1 mark]*. However, during the summer, there will be more daylight hours and the weather will be less windy *[1 mark]*, so solar panels will be more favourable *[1 mark]*. By installing both, the university will have a more reliable electricity supply throughout the year *[1 mark]*.

4.1   How to grade your answer:
Level 0:   There is no relevant information. *[No marks]*
Level 1:   There is a brief description of the reliability or environmental impact of one of the energy resources. *[1 to 2 marks]*
Level 2:   There is a clear and detailed description of the reliability and environmental impacts of both energy resources, as well as some similarities between them. *[3 to 4 marks]*
Here are some points your answer may include:
Both energy resources are reliable.
Tides come in and out at known times.
Except in times of drought, there is always water available for a hydroelectric power plant to work.
Hydroelectric power plants require the flooding of valleys, which causes a loss of habitat for any animals living there.
The plants in the valley die during the flood and rot, which releases gases that contribute to global warming.
Using tides to generate electricity creates no pollution, but tidal barrages do alter the habitat of nearby animals.

4.2   How to grade your answer:
Level 0:   There is no relevant information. *[No marks]*
Level 1:   There is a brief explanation of an advantage or a disadvantage of fossil fuels. *[1 to 2 marks]*
Level 2:   There is some explanation of both advantages and disadvantages of fossil fuels. *[3 to 4 marks]*
Level 3:   There is a clear and detailed explanation of the advantages and disadvantages of using fossil fuels. *[5 to 6 marks]*
Here are some points your answer may include:
Advantages:
Fossil fuels are reliable.
They are extracted at a fast enough rate that there are always some in stock.
Power plants can respond quickly to peaks in demand.
Running costs of fossil fuel power plants aren't that expensive compared to other energy resources.
Fuel extraction costs are also low.

Disadvantages:
Fossil fuels are slowly running out / they are a non-renewable energy resource.
Burning fossil fuels releases carbon dioxide into the atmosphere.
Carbon dioxide in the atmosphere contributes to global warming.
Burning coal and oil also releases sulfur dioxide, which causes acid rain.
Acid rain can damage soil and trees. This can damage or destroy the habitats of animals.
Coal mining can spoil the view by damaging the landscape.
Oil spillages kill sea life and birds and mammals that live near to the sea.

Page 12 — Trends in Energy Resource Use

1.1 $35 + 23 + 5 = 63 \%$
[2 marks for correct answer, otherwise 1 mark for reading all three values correctly from the graph]

1.2   E.g. the country is using a larger percentage renewable energy resources to generate electricity in 2015 than they were the previous year / overall, they are using a smaller percentage of fossil fuels to generate their electricity in 2015 than they were in 2014 *[1 mark]*.

2   How to grade your answer:
Level 0:   There is no relevant information. *[No marks]*
Level 1:   There is a brief explanation why the UK is using more renewable energy resources.
[1 to 2 marks]
Level 2:   There is some explanation of why the UK is using more renewable energy resources and the factors that restrict the increase in their use.
[3 to 4 marks]
Level 3:   There is a clear and detailed explanation of why the UK is using more renewable energy resources and the factors that restrict the increase in their use. *[5 to 6 marks]*
Here are some points your answer may include:
Reasons the UK is using more renewable energy resources:
We understand more about the negative effects that fossil fuels have on the environment, so more people want to use renewable energy resources that have less of an impact on the environment.
Fossil fuel reserves will run out, so we have to find an alternative for them.
Pressure from the public and other countries has lead to government targets for the use of renewable energy resources. This can lead to increased government funding for renewable energy resources.
Pressure from the public and the global community/other countries has also lead to private companies creating more environmentally-friendly products that use renewable energy resources.
Factors that limit the use of renewable energy resources:
Building new power plants to replace existing fossil fuel powered ones costs money.
Some renewable energy resources are less reliable than fossil fuels.
Research into improving renewable energy resources costs money and will take time.
Personal products that use renewable energy resources, like hybrid cars, are generally more expensive than similar ones that use fossil fuels.

Topic 2 — Electricity

Page 13 — Current and Circuit Symbols

Warm-up
A — cell, B — switch, C — filament lamp, D — fuse.
1.1   There is no source of potential difference *[1 mark]*
1.2   Current is the rate of flow of **charge** *[1 mark]*.
2.1   0.5 A *[1 mark]*
Remember that the current is the same at any point in a single closed circuit loop.
2.2 $Q = I \times t$ *[1 mark]*
2.3 $t = 2 \times 60 = 120$ s
Charge $= 0.5 \times 120$ *[1 mark]* $= \mathbf{60}$ *[1 mark]* C *[1 mark]*

Page 14 — Resistance and V = IR

1    $V = I \times R$
$V = 3 \times 6$ *[1 mark]* $= \mathbf{18}$ V *[1 mark]*
2.1   She could have varied the length of the wire between the crocodile clips *[1 mark]* and divided the reading on the voltmeter by the reading on the ammeter to find the resistance for each length *[1 mark]*.
2.2

[graph: Resistance (Ω) on vertical axis from 0 to 3.0, Length (cm) on horizontal axis from 0 to 50, with plotted points and a straight line of best fit through the origin]

[1 mark for resistance on vertical axis and length on horizontal axis, 1 mark for appropriate values labelled on both axes, 1 mark for correctly plotted points, 1 mark for suitable line of best fit.]

2.3   The resistance is proportional to the length *[1 mark]*. This is shown by the graph being a straight line through the origin *[1 mark]*.

Pages 15-16 — Resistance and I-V Characteristics

1.1   C *[1 mark]*
At a constant temperature, the relationship between pd and current is linear — when this is true, the resistor is said to be ohmic.
1.2   I-V characteristic *[1 mark]*
1.3   A resistor at a constant temperature is an example of an **ohmic** conductor. It is also an example of a **linear** component.
[1 mark for each correct answer]
2.1

[diode symbol] *[1 mark]*

2.2   A diode only lets current flow through it in one direction *[1 mark]*.
2.3   The student put the diode/power supply in the circuit the other way around *[1 mark]*. The resistance of a diode is very large when current goes through it one way and very small when current goes through in the opposite direction *[1 mark]*.
3.1   It is used to alter the current *[1 mark]* so the potential difference can be measured for each current *[1 mark]*.
3.2   At 3 A the pd is 12 V *[1 mark]*
$V = I \times R$
$R = V \div I$ *[1 mark]* $= 12 \div 3$ *[1 mark]* $= 4\ \Omega$ *[1 mark]*
3.3   The resistance increases as the current increases *[1 mark]*. This is because the increase in current causes the temperature to rise *[1 mark]*.
3.4   A resistor is ohmic when the relationship between current and potential difference is linear *[1 mark]*. The graph is linear until approximately 3.5 V, so the resistor is ohmic in this range *[1 mark]*.

Page 17 — Circuit Devices

1.1

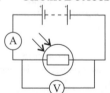

[1 mark for correct LDR symbol, 1 mark for LDR, ammeter and power supply in series, 1 mark for voltmeter in parallel across LDR.]

1.2   It decreases *[1 mark]*
1.3   E.g. automatic night lights / burglar detectors *[1 mark]*
2   As the temperature increases, the resistance of the thermistor decreases *[1 mark]*. This means the current in the circuit

increases *[1 mark]*. As the current increases, the brightness of the light increases *[1 mark]*. When the cooker's surface is cold, the resistance is high and the current is too small to light the bulb *[1 mark]*.

Page 18 — Series Circuits

1   A *[1 mark]*.

In a series circuit, there should only be one closed loop of wire.

2.1 $10 + 30 = \textbf{40 } \boldsymbol{\Omega}$ *[1 mark]*

2.2 $V = I \times R$

        $V = 75 \times 10^{-3} \times 30$ *[1 mark]* = **2.25 V** *[1 mark]*

3   The potential difference across the 8 Ω resistor is:

      $6 - 2 = 4$ V *[1 mark]*

      $V = I \times R$, so the current through the 8 Ω resistor is:

      $I = V \div R = 4 \div 8$ *[1 mark]* = 0.5 A *[1 mark]*

      This is the same as the current through R, so the resistance of R is: $R = V \div I = 2 \div 0.5$ *[1 mark]* = **4 Ω** *[1 mark]*

Page 19 — Parallel Circuits

1

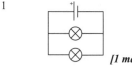

      [1 mark]

2.1   6 V *[1 mark]*

Potential difference is the same across all components in parallel.

2.2 $V = IR$ so $I = V \div R$ *[1 mark]*

      $A_1: I = V \div R = 6 \div 4$ *[1 mark]* = **1.5 A** *[1 mark]*

      $A_2: I = V \div R = 6 \div 12$ *[1 mark]* = **0.5 A** *[1 mark]*

2.3   The current from the supply splits into 1.5 A and 0.5 A.

      So A_3 reads $1.5 + 0.5 = $ **2 A** *[1 mark]*

3   How to grade your answer:

      Level 0:   There is no relevant information. *[No marks]*

      Level 1:   There is a brief explanation about the effect of adding resistors in series or parallel. *[1 to 2 marks]*

      Level 2:   There is a comparison between adding resistors in series and parallel and an explanation of their effects. *[3 to 4 marks]*

      Level 3:   A logical and detailed comparison is given, explaining why adding resistors in series increases the total resistance but adding them in parallel reduces it. *[5 to 6 marks]*

      Here are some points your answer may include:

      In series, resistors share the potential difference from the power source.

      The more resistors that are in series, the lower the potential difference for each one, and so the lower the current for each one.

      Current is the same all around a series circuit, so adding a resistor will decrease the current for the whole circuit.

      A decrease in total current means an increase in total resistance.

      In parallel, all resistors have the same potential difference as the source.

      Adding another resistor in parallel (forming another circuit loop) increases the current flowing in the circuit, as there are more paths for the current to flow through.

      An increase in total current means a decrease in total resistance (because $V = IR$).

Page 20 — Investigating Resistance

1.1

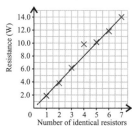

Resistance = **8.0 Ω**

[1 mark for a straight line of best fit that excludes the point plotted for 4 resistors, 1 mark for correct prediction of resistance]

1.2

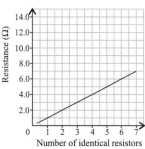

[1 mark for a straight line of best fit with a positive gradient, 1 mark for the gradient of the line being half of the gradient of the line drawn in 1.1]

2   How to grade your answer:

      Level 0:   There is no relevant information. *[No marks]*

      Level 1:   There is a brief description of the techniques used to measure resistance of the circuit. The steps mentioned are not in a logical order. *[1 to 2 marks]*

      Level 2:   There is a good description of the techniques used to measure resistance of the circuit. Most steps are given in a logical order and they could be followed to produced valid results. A correct circuit diagram may be included. *[3 to 4 marks]*

      Level 3:   A logical and detailed description is given, fully describing the method for investigating the effect of adding resistors in parallel. The method could easily be followed to produce valid results. A correct circuit diagram may be included. *[5 to 6 marks]*

      Here are some points your answer may include:

      Connect a battery or cell in series with an ammeter and a fixed resistor.

      Measure the source potential difference using the voltmeter.

      Measure the current through the circuit using the ammeter.

      Calculate the resistance of the circuit using $R = V \div I$.

      Connect a second identical resistor in parallel with the first resistor.

      Do not connect the second resistor across the ammeter.

      Measure the current and use this to calculate the resistance of the circuit.

      Repeat this for several identical resistors.

      Plot a graph of number of identical resistors against overall resistance of the circuit.

      A correct circuit diagram, similar to:

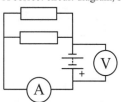

So long as you draw a correct diagram with at least two resistors in parallel, you would get the marks. You could also draw your circuit with several resistors in parallel, all separated with switches.

Page 21 — Electricity in the Home

Warm-up

The live wire is **brown** and is at a potential difference of **230** V.

The earth wire is **green and yellow** and is at a potential difference of **0** V.

1.1   230 V *[1 mark]*

      50 Hz *[1 mark]*

1.2   How to grade your answer:

      Level 0:   There is no relevant information. *[No marks]*

      Level 1:   There is a brief explanation of the function of the live and neutral wires and some attempt at explaining why the toaster would not work. *[1 to 2 marks]*

      Level 2:   There is a good explanation of the function of the live and neutral wires and why the fault would not

allow a current to flow through the toaster.
[3 to 4 marks]
Here are some points your answer may include:
The purpose of the neutral wire is to complete the circuit.
Current flows into the toaster via the live wire, through the toaster, and out of the device by the neutral wire.
The fault means that a closed loop/low-resistance path has been formed between the live and neutral wire before the current in the live wire has reached the toaster.
So no (or very little) current will flow through the toaster.
This means that the toaster will not work.

2.1 To stop an electric current from flowing out of the live wire and potentially causing an electric shock (i.e. for safety) *[1 mark]*. To make it easy to identify the live wire *[1 mark]*.
2.2 The man has an electric potential of 0 V *[1 mark]* and the wire has an electric potential (of 230 V) so a potential difference exists between them *[1 mark]*. This causes a current to flow through the man *[1 mark]*.
2.3 Yes *[1 mark]*. Although there is no current flowing when it is switched off, there is still a potential difference *[1 mark]*, so touching the live wire in the socket could cause a current to flow through you to the Earth *[1 mark]*.

Page 22 — Power of Electrical Appliances

1 The **power** of an appliance is the energy transferred **per second**. Energy is transferred because the **current** does work against the appliance's resistance. *[1 mark for each correct]*
2.1 $E = P \times t$ *[1 mark]*
2.2 $E = 50 \times 20$ *[1 mark]* = **1000 J** *[1 mark]*
2.3 The power of the car is higher *[1 mark]*. So more energy is transferred away from the chemical energy store of the battery per second *[1 mark]*.
3.1 Energy is transferred electrically from the power source *[1 mark]* to the thermal energy store of the water *[1 mark]* and the kinetic energy store of the motor *[1 mark]*.
3.2 Work done = power × time ($E = P \times t$)
Work done = 400×60 *[1 mark]* = **24 000 J** *[1 mark]*
3.3 Time of economy mode = $160 \times 60 = 9600$ s
Energy transferred in economy mode
= power × time = $400 \times 9600 = 3\,840\,000$ J *[1 mark]*
Time of standard mode = $125 \times 60 = 7500$ s
Energy transferred in standard mode = 600×7500
= $4\,500\,000$ J *[1 mark]*
Energy saved = $4\,500\,000 - 3\,840\,000$ *[1 mark]*
= **660 000 J** *[1 mark]*

Page 23 — More on Power

Warm-up
A power source supplies **energy** to a charge. When a charge passes through a component with **resistance**, it does **work**, so the charge's energy **decreases**.
1.1 $E = V \times Q$ *[1 mark]*
1.2 $E = 6 \times 2$ *[1 mark]* = **12 J** *[1 mark]*
1.3 Multiplying the potential difference by the current gives the power *[1 mark]*. In 1.2 the energy was transferred by the two coulombs of charge in one second *[1 mark]*. This is the same as the power *[1 mark]*.
2.1 $P = I \times V$
so $I = P \div V = 75 \div 230$ *[1 mark]* = 0.3260...
= **0.33 A (to 2 s.f.)** *[1 mark]*
2.2 $P = I^2 \times R$
so $R = P \div I^2 = 2.5 \div 0.50^2$ *[1 mark]* = **10 Ω** *[1 mark]*

Page 24 — The National Grid

1.1 Potential Difference *[1 mark]*, Current *[1 mark]*
1.2 A step-up transformer increases the potential difference, a step-down transformer decreases it *[1 mark]*.
2.1 Transformer A = step-up transformer *[1 mark]*
Transformer B = step-down transformer *[1 mark]*
2.2 How to grade your answer:
Level 0: There is no relevant information. *[No marks]*
Level 1: There is a brief explanation of the function of the step-up transformer and how this results in smaller energy losses. *[1 to 2 marks]*

Level 2: There is a good explanation of the function of the step-up transformer and how reducing the energy lost increases the efficiency of the national grid.
[3 to 4 marks]
Here are some points your answer may include:
Transformer A increases the potential difference.
This decreases the current at a given power.
This decrease in current decreases energy lost to the thermal energy stores of the cables and surroundings.
Efficiency is useful output energy transfer ÷ total input energy transfer, so reducing the energy lost to thermal stores makes the transmission of electricity more efficient.
2.3 The potential difference across the power cables is very high and too large for domestic devices *[1 mark]*. Transformer B reduces the potential difference to lower, usable levels *[1 mark]*.

Page 25 — Static Electricity

1.1 The charges are alike *[1 mark]*. The balloons are repelling each other *[1 mark]*.
1.2 The balloons were rubbed against something,
e.g. clothing/hair *[1 mark]*.
This wouldn't work if the balloons were rubbed against each other, as that would charge them up with opposite charges
2.1 Electrons *[1 mark]* are removed from the dusting cloth and transferred to the polythene rod *[1 mark]*.
2.2 The student could bring the dusting cloth towards one end of the rod *[1 mark]*. The rod should turn towards the cloth *[1 mark]*.
3.1 The man is charged, so there is a potential difference between him and the rail *[1 mark]*. When the potential difference is high enough, electrons jump across the gap to the rail, producing a spark *[1 mark]*.
3.2 Negatively charged *[1 mark]*. Only negative charges/electrons can move *[1 mark]* and they will move from an area of negative charge to an earthed area *[1 mark]*.

Page 26 — Electric Fields

1.1

[1 mark]
1.2 A region in which a charged object will experience a force *[1 mark]*.
1.3 It decreases *[1 mark]*.
1.4 The second sphere is not charged *[1 mark]*.
2.1 The size of the force increases *[1 mark]*.
2.2 The negative charges are attracted towards the positive sphere, while the positive charges are attracted towards the negative sphere *[1 mark]*. So parts of the particle are pulled away from each other *[1 mark]*. When the potential difference is high enough, the force becomes large enough to break the particle apart *[1 mark]*.

Topic 3 — Particle Model of Matter

Pages 27-28 — Density of Materials

Warm-up
From left to right: liquid, solid, gas
1.1 $\rho = m \div v$ *[1 mark]*
1.2 $\rho = 10\,000 \div 0.5$ *[1 mark]* = **20 000 kg/m³** *[1 mark]*
1.3 The density is the same for the whole block,
so $\rho = 20\,000$ kg/m³
$\rho = m \div v$ so $m = \rho \times v$ *[1 mark]*
= $20\,000 \times 0.02$ *[1 mark]* = **400 kg** *[1 mark]*
2 There is a smaller mass (and so fewer particles) in a given volume of ice than of water *[1 mark]*. So the water molecules are further apart in ice than they are in liquid water *[1 mark]*.
Substances are usually more dense as a solid than as a liquid,
but water is an exception to this.
3.1 How to grade your answer:
Level 0: There is no relevant information. *[No marks]*
Level 1: There is a brief description of how to measure the mass of the object and how to use this along with its

volume to calculate its density. *[1 to 2 marks]*

Level 2:   There is a clear description of how to measure both the mass and volume of the object and how to use these values to calculate its density. *[3 to 4 marks]*

Here are some points your answer may include:
First measure the mass of the object using a mass balance.
Then submerge the object in the water.
Measure the volume of water displaced using the scale on the measuring cylinder.
The volume of the displaced water in the measuring cylinder is equal to the volume of the object.
Use density = mass ÷ volume to calculate the density of the object.

3.2 $\rho = m \div v$
1 ml of water = 1 cm³ *[1 mark]*
A: $\rho = 5.7 \div 0.30 = 19$ g/cm³. So A is gold. *[1 mark]*
B: $\rho = 2.7 \div 0.60 = 4.5$ g/cm³. So B is titanium. *[1 mark]*
C: $\rho = 3.0 \div 0.30 = 10$ g/cm³. So C is silver. *[1 mark]*

4   Volume of empty aluminium can
= volume displaced by full can − volume of cola
= 337 − 332 = 5 ml *[1 mark]*
5 ml = 5 cm³ *[1 mark]*
$\rho = m \div v = 13.5 \div 5$ *[1 mark]* = **2.7 g/cm³** *[1 mark]*

Page 29 — Internal Energy and Changes of State

1   When a system is heated, the internal energy of the system **increases**. This either increases the **temperature** of the system or causes a change of state. During a change of state the temperature and **mass** of the substance remain constant.
[2 marks for all correct, otherwise 1 mark for two correct]

2.1   Gas to liquid: condensing
Liquid to gas: evaporating/boiling
[1 mark for both correct]

2.2   E.g. a change where you don't end up with a new substance / you end up with the same substance in a different form *[1 mark]*.

3.1   E.g. the energy stored in a system by its particles. / The sum of the energy in the particles' kinetic and potential energy stores *[1 mark]*.

3.2   Any two from: mass, specific heat capacity, total energy transferred to the system *[2 marks]*

4   10 g *[1 mark]* E.g. because when a substance changes state, its mass doesn't change. So the mass of the water vapour equals the mass of the water originally in the test tube *[1 mark]*.

Page 30 — Specific Latent Heat

1.1   The amount of energy required to change the state of one kilogram of a substance with no change in temperature *[1 mark]*.

1.2 $E = mL$ so $L = E \div m$ *[1 mark]*
$L = 1.13 \div 0.5$ *[1 mark]* = **2.26 MJ/kg** *[1 mark]*

2.1   The substance is melting *[1 mark]*.

2.2   As the substance is heated, its internal energy increases *[1 mark]*. As the substance melts (during 3-8 minutes), all of this energy is used to break apart intermolecular bonds *[1 mark]* so there is no increase in the substance's temperature as it changes state *[1 mark]*.

2.3   Melting point = −7 °C *[1 mark]*
Boiling point = 58 °C *[1 mark]*

Pages 31-32 — Particle Motion in Gases

Warm-up
They are constantly moving in random directions at random speeds.

1   When the temperature of a gas increases, the average energy in the **kinetic** energy stores of the gas molecules increases. This **increases** the **average** speed of the gas molecules. If the gas is kept at a constant volume, increasing the temperature **increases** the pressure.
[3 marks for all correct, otherwise 1 mark for two correct or 2 marks for three correct]

2.1 $pV = $ constant
$8.0 \times 10^{-4} \times 50 \times 10^3 = 40$ *[1 mark]*
So $p = 40 \div (1.6 \times 10^{-4})$ *[1 mark]* = 250 000 = **250 kPa** *[1 mark]*

2.2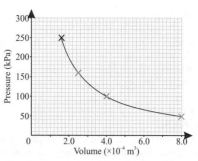

[1 mark for correctly plotted point, 1 mark for a curved line connecting them]

3   E.g. a gas is made of particles *[1 mark]*. The particles collide with each other and the sides of the container they are in, which exerts a force on the sides of the container *[1 mark]*. The total force per unit area exerted on the container is the gas pressure *[1 mark]*. As the volume is increased, the gas particles spread out more *[1 mark]*. This means that there are fewer collisions with the sides of the container in a given time, so the pressure is lower *[1 mark]*.

4   How to grade your answer:
Level 0:   There is no relevant information. *[No marks]*
Level 1:   There is a brief explanation of how work is done on the air. *[1 to 2 marks]*
Level 2:   There is some explanation of how doing work on the air increases its temperature. *[3 to 4 marks]*
Level 3:   There is a clear and detailed explanation of how doing work on the air transfers energy to the particles in the air and how it causes an increase in temperature. *[5 to 6 marks]*

Here are some points your answer may include:
To compress the air, work must be done.
This work is done against the force caused by the pressure of the air in the piston.
Doing work causes a transfer of energy.
Energy is transferred to the internal energy of the system.
So energy is transferred to the kinetic energy stores of the air particles in the system.
This increases the temperature of the air/gas.
Because temperature of a gas is related to the average energy in the kinetic energy stores of the gas molecules.
So doing work on the gas increases its temperature.

Topic 4 — Atomic Structure

Pages 33-34 — Developing the Model of the Atom

Warm-up
1×10^{-10} m
10 000

1.1   Our current model shows that the atom can be broken up (into protons, neutrons and electrons) *[1 mark]*.

1.2   The plum pudding model *[1 mark]*. This was where an atom was thought to be a sphere of positive charge, with electrons spread throughout it *[1 mark]*.

1.3   The neutron *[1 mark]*.

2.1   An electron can move into a higher energy level / further from the nucleus, by absorbing EM radiation *[1 mark]*, and move into a lower energy level / closer to the nucleus, by emitting EM radiation *[1 mark]*.

2.2   ion *[1 mark]*

2.3   Positive (or +1) *[1 mark]*
An atom is neutral. Losing an electron takes away negative charge, so the remaining ion is positive.

3   Level 0:   There is no relevant information. *[No marks]*
Level 1:   There is only one correct discovery mentioned with a brief description of the observation that led to it. *[1 to 2 marks]*
Level 2:   Two correct discoveries are given with a detailed description of how observations led to them. *[3 to 4 marks]*

Here are some points your answer may include:
Discovery: The atom is mostly made up of empty space / most of the atom's mass is concentrated at the centre in a tiny nucleus.
Observation: Most of the alpha particles fired at the thin gold foil passed straight through.
Discovery: The atom has a positively charged central nucleus.
Observation: Some of the positive alpha particles were deflected back towards the emitter, so they were repelled by the nucleus.

4.1 Proton: (+)1 *[1 mark]*
Neutron: 0 *[1 mark]*

4.2 The protons and neutrons are in the central nucleus *[1 mark]* and the electrons surround the nucleus (arranged in shells) *[1 mark]*.

4.3 26 electrons *[1 mark]*. Atoms are neutral *[1 mark]*. Protons and electrons have equal but opposite charges. For these charges to cancel, there must be the same number of each *[1 mark]*.

Pages 35-36 — Isotopes and Nuclear Radiation
Warm-up
Gamma — weakly ionising, alpha — strongly ionising, beta — moderately ionising.

1.1 radioactive decay *[1 mark]*
1.2 Atoms with the same number of protons *[1 mark]* but different numbers of neutrons (in their nuclei) *[1 mark]*.
1.3 An atom losing (or gaining) at least one electron *[1 mark]*.
1.4 Alpha decay *[1 mark]*
2 E.g. Alpha particles have a small range in air and will be stopped by a thin sheet of material *[1 mark]*. So the alpha radiation inside the detector cannot escape the detector *[1 mark]*.

3.1 23 *[1 mark]*
Remember that the mass number is the little number in the top-left. It's the total number of protons and neutrons in the nucleus.
3.2 23 – 11 = 12 neutrons *[1 mark]*
The number of neutrons is the difference between the mass number and the atomic number.
3.3 $^{24}_{11}$Na *[1 mark]*
An isotope has the same number of protons (so the same atomic number), but a different number of neutrons (so a different mass number).
3.4 The atomic number of the neon isotope is lower, so there are fewer protons in the neon isotope *[1 mark]*. So the charge on the neon isotope's nucleus is lower than the charge on the sodium isotope's nucleus *[1 mark]*.

4 How to grade your answer:
Level 0: There is no relevant information. *[No marks]*
Level 1: There is a brief explanation of the method of locating the leak and of the radiation used. *[1 to 2 marks]*
Level 2: There is some explanation of the method of locating the leak and of the radiation used. *[3 to 4 marks]*
Level 3: There is a clear and detailed explanation of the method of locating the leak and of the radiation used. *[5 to 6 marks]*
Here are some points your answer may include:
The isotope travels along the pipe.
If there is no leak, the radiation doesn't escape the pipe/not much radiation can escape the pipe/some of the radiation is blocked by the pipe.
If there is a leak, the isotope escapes the pipe and some/more radiation can reach the detector.
This causes the count-rate to increase.
An increase in count-rate indicates a leak.
The isotope could be beta-emitting because beta radiation would be blocked by the pipe but would not be blocked by the small amount of ground above the pipe.
OR The isotope could be gamma-emitting because it can escape the pipe and reach the detector, and more gamma radiation would get to the detector if there was a leak.

Page 37 — Nuclear Equations
1.1 It increases the positive charge on the nucleus / makes the nucleus 'more positive' *[1 mark]*.
1.2 The atomic number increases *[1 mark]* but the mass number stays the same *[1 mark]*. This is because emitting an electron (beta decay) involves a neutron turning into a proton *[1 mark]*.

Remember that a neutron turns into a proton in order to increase the positive charge on the nucleus. (Because emitting the electron has taken away some negative charge.)
1.3 No effect *[1 mark]*
When an electron moves to a lower energy level, it loses energy in the form of an EM wave, which doesn't change the charge or mass of the nucleus.
2.1 The atomic numbers on each side are not equal *[1 mark]*.
2.2 $^{0}_{-1}$e *[1 mark]*
The other particle must be an electron (a beta particle), as this will balance the equation.
2.3 $^{226}_{88}$Ra $\longrightarrow$ $^{222}_{86}$Rn + $^{4}_{2}$He
[3 marks in total — 1 mark for each correct symbol]
You know that the mass number of the radium is 226 (that's what 'radium-226' means). You also know that an alpha particle is $^{4}_{2}$He, so you can find the mass and atomic numbers of radon by balancing the equation.
2.4 Rn-222 has 222 – 86 = 136 neutrons *[1 mark]*
2 alpha decays = 2 × 2 = 4 neutrons released *[1 mark]*
136 – 4 = **132** *[1 mark]*

Pages 38-39 — Half-life
1.1 E.g. the time taken for the count-rate of a sample to halve *[1 mark]*.
1.2 75 seconds *[1 mark]*
The initial count-rate is 60 cps. Half of this is 30 cps, which corresponds to 75 seconds on the time axis.
1.3 After 1 half-life, there will be 800 ÷ 2 = 400 undecayed nuclei remaining. After 2 half-lives, there will be 400 ÷ 2 = 200 undecayed nuclei remaining. So 800 – 200 = **600** nuclei will have decayed.
[2 marks for correct answer, otherwise 1 mark for calculating the number of decayed/undecayed nuclei after one half-life]
1.4 After 2 half-lives, there are 200 undecayed nuclei.
The ratio is 200:800,
which simplifies to **1:4** *[1 mark]*
You don't even need the numbers to work out this ratio. For any radioactive isotope, after two half lives, the initial number of undecayed nuclei will have halved and then halved again. It will be one quarter of the original number, so the ratio is always 1:4.
2 Isotope 1, because more nuclei will decay per second *[1 mark]*.
3.1 It takes a total of 2 hours and 30 minutes for the activity to halve from 8800 Bq to 4400 Bq,
so its half-life = (2 × 60) + 30 = **150 minutes** *[1 mark]*
3.2 Check how many half-lives pass during 6 hours and 15 minutes:
6 hours and 15 minutes = (6 × 60) + 15 = 375 minutes
375 ÷ 150 = 2.5 half-lives
The activity can only be worked out if a whole number of half-lives have passed, so calculate how many half-lives have passed from the time when activity = 6222 Bq:
1 hour 15 minutes = 60 + 15 = 75 minutes
375 – 75 = 300 minutes
300 ÷ 150 = 2 half-lives.
So now you can calculate the activity after 2 half-lives, with an initial activity of 6222 Bq:
After 1 half-life, the activity will be 6222 ÷ 2 = 3111 Bq
After 2 half-lives, the activity will be 3111 ÷ 2 = 1555.5 Bq
1555.5 = **1600 Bq (to 2 s.f.)**
[2 marks for correct answer, otherwise 1 mark for finding how many half-lives will have passed between 1 hour and 15 minutes and 6 hours and 15 minutes]
4.1

[3 marks in total — 2 marks for all points plotted correctly, otherwise 1 mark for three points plotted correctly, 1 mark for smooth curve.]

Start the graph at 120 Bq. After 50 s, this will have halved to 60 Bq. After another 50 s (i.e. 100 s altogether), it will have halved again, to 30 Bq. Plot these points, then join them up with a nice smooth curve.

4.2   70 Bq (accept between 68 Bq and 72 Bq)
          [1 mark for correct value from your graph]

4.3   After 200 s, 15 ÷ 2 = 7.5 Bq
          After 250 s, 7.5 ÷ 2 = **3.75 Bq** *[1 mark]*
          E.g. radioactive decay is random *[1 mark]* and the effect of randomness on the activity will be greater for lower activities *[1 mark]*.

Pages 40-41 — Background Radiation and Contamination

Warm-up

E.g. cosmic rays / rocks

1   Any two from: e.g. using shielding / working in a different room to the radioactive source / using remote-controlled arms to handle sources / wearing protective suits *[2 marks]*

2.1   Low-level radiation which is around us all of the time. *[1 mark]*

2.2   Systematic error *[1 mark]*. If she doesn't subtract the background radiation, her results will all be too large by the same amount *[1 mark]*.

This assumes that the background level is constant for the duration of her experiment. This is a reasonable assumption, as long as she carries out the experiment in the same location under the same conditions each time.

2.3   Radiation dose *[1 mark]*

2.4   E.g. Where you live / your job *[1 mark for both correct]*

3.1   Contamination is when unwanted radioactive particles get onto an object *[1 mark]*. Irradiation is when an object is exposed to radiation *[1 mark]*.

3.2   E.g. keeping the sample in a protective box / standing behind a protective barrier *[1 mark]*

3.3   Any two from: e.g. wearing protective gloves / using tongs / wearing a protective suit or mask *[2 marks]*.

4   How to grade your answer:
          Level 0:   There is no relevant information. *[No marks]*
          Level 1:   There is a brief explanation of the dangers of contamination or radiation. *[1 to 2 marks]*
          Level 2:   There is some explanation of the dangers and risks of contamination and radiation. *[3 to 4 marks]*
          Level 3:   There is a clear and detailed explanation of the dangers and risks of contamination and radiation, used to justify the conclusion that the clockmaker should be more concerned about contamination. *[5 to 6 marks]*

Here are some points your answer may include:
Alpha particles are strongly ionising.
Alpha particles are stopped by skin or thin paper.
Being irradiated won't make the clockmaker radioactive.
But irradiation may do some damage to his skin.
However, the radiation cannot penetrate his body and cause damage to his tissue or organs.
If the clockmaker's hands get contaminated with radium-226, he will be exposed to more alpha particles, close to his skin. Or he may accidentally ingest (eat) some.
Or if particles of the radium get into the air, he could breathe them in.
The radium will then decay whilst inside his body.
This means that the alpha particles can do lots of damage to nearby tissue or organs.
So he should be more concerned about contamination.

Page 42 — Uses and Risk

Warm-up

Radiation can cause cells to **mutate** or **die**, which can cause cancer or radiation sickness. Radiation can also be used to treat **cancer** and to **diagnose** illnesses.

1.1   Gamma *[1 mark]*

1.2   E.g. the gamma rays could cause damage to healthy cells *[1 mark]*. Rotating the beam ensures healthy cells nearby get a lower dose of radiation *[1 mark]*.

2.1   Iodine-123 could be injected into or swallowed by the patient, where it would be absorbed by their thyroid *[1 mark]*. The

iodine would then decay, giving off radiation that could be detected outside the body *[1 mark]*. The amount of radiation detected could then be used to find how much iodine has been absorbed by the thyroid, to check whether or not the thyroid is overactive *[1 mark]*.

2.2   Because alpha radiation would be too dangerous inside the body *[1 mark]* and it would not be detectable outside the body, as it cannot penetrate tissue *[1 mark]*.

2.3   A short half-life means the activity will quickly drop, so the patient will not be exposed to radiation for too long *[1 mark]*.

Page 43 — Fission and Fusion

1   Both statements are true *[1 mark]*.

2   Similarity: E.g. they both release energy *[1 mark]*.
          Difference: E.g. fission is the splitting of a large nucleus to form a smaller nuclei, whereas fusion is the joining of smaller nuclei to form a larger one *[1 mark]*.

3.1   How to grade your answer:
          Level 0:   There is no relevant information. *[No marks]*
          Level 1:   There is a brief explanation of nuclear fission and that a neutron can start the fission reaction. *[1 to 2 marks]*
          Level 2:   There is a detailed explanation of how a neutron starts a forced fission reaction, what a fission reaction is and how this leads to a chain reaction. *[3 to 4 marks]*

Here are some points your answer may include:
Absorbing a neutron makes the nucleus more unstable.
The unstable nucleus undergoes fission.
Fission is the splitting of an unstable nucleus into two lighter elements and releasing two or three neutrons.
These neutrons can be absorbed by other nuclei, causing more fission.
Each decay can cause another decay to happen, which is a chain reaction.

3.2   E.g. each fission decay releases energy *[1 mark]* so an uncontrolled chain reaction would release lots of energy, which could lead to reactor meltdown/an explosion *[1 mark]*.

Topic 5 — Forces

Page 44 — Contact and Non-Contact Forces

Warm-up

Scalar — mass, time, temperature
Vector — acceleration, weight, force

1   Vector quantities have both magnitude and direction. *[1 mark]*

2   Contact force: e.g. friction / tension / normal contact force / air resistance *[1 mark]*
          Non-contact force: e.g. weight / gravitational force *[1 mark]*

3.1

      [1 mark for correct arrow length, 1 mark for correct direction]

3.2   Both arrows need to be longer (to indicate the stronger interaction) *[1 mark]*
          The arrows need to be the same size as each other *[1 mark]*.

Page 45 — Weight, Mass and Gravity

1   **Mass** is the amount of matter in an object. **Weight** is a force due to gravity. Mass is measured **kilograms** whilst weight is measured in **newtons**. The weight of an object is **directly** proportional to its mass. *[3 marks for all correct, 2 marks for 3-4 correct, 1 mark for 1-2 correct]*

2   A point at which you can assume the whole mass of an object is concentrated. / The point from which the weight of an object can be assumed to act. *[1 mark]*

3.1 $W = mg$ *[1 mark]*

3.2 $W = 350 \times 9.8$ *[1 mark]* = **3430 N** *[1 mark]*

3.3   New mass = 350 − 209 = 141 kg *[1 mark]*
          $W = mg = 141 \times 3.8$ *[1 mark]* = 535.8
                              = **536 N (to 3 s.f.)** *[1 mark]*

10

Page 46 — Resultant Forces and Work Done

1   C *[1 mark]*

The resultant force is the sum of the two forces acting on each runner, taking into account the direction. For runner C, the resultant force is 130 N − 100 N = 30 N.

2.1 $W = Fs = 50 \times 15$ *[1 mark]* = **750** *[1 mark]*
         Unit: **J** or **Nm** *[1 mark]*

2.2   The temperature of the suitcase increases *[1 mark]* because doing work causes some energy to be transferred to the thermal energy store of the suitcase *[1 mark]*.

3.1   100 N *[1 mark]*

As the ladder isn't moving, the resultant force is zero, and so the weight of the ladder is equal to the normal contact force acting on the ladder.

3.2

[1 mark for correct arrow length (same as 30 N arrow length), 1 mark for correct direction]

Page 47 — Calculating Forces

Warm-up
Horizontal component = 4 N
Vertical component = 3 N

1.1   1 cm = 100 N *[1 mark]*

1.2

Magnitude = **430 N**
[1 mark for correct construction of resultant force, 1 mark for correct magnitude]

Page 48 — Forces and Elasticity

1.1   Elastic deformation is when an object returns to its original size after the deforming force is removed *[1 mark]*. Inelastic deformation is when an object has been deformed such that it cannot return to its original size or shape after the deforming force is removed *[1 mark]*.

1.2   Compressing, bending *[1 mark for both correct]*

2.1 $F = ke$ so $k = F \div e$
         $e = 20$ cm = 0.2 m
         so $k = 250 \div 0.2$ *[1 mark]* = **1250** *[1 mark]*
         Unit = **N/m** *[1 mark]*

2.2   E.g. Agree — the extension will be 40 cm, because force is proportional to extension, so doubling the force doubles the extension *[1 mark]*, assuming that the spring hasn't gone past its limit of proportionality *[1 mark]*.

Page 49 — Investigating Springs

1.1

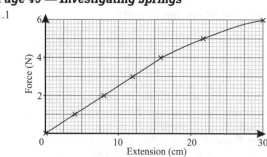

[1 mark for points plotted correctly, 1 mark for line of best fit showing linear relationship at the start, 1 mark for curved line of best fit towards the end of the graph]

1.2   Spring constant = Force ÷ Extension
         = gradient of the linear section of the graph
         $k = 3 \div 0.12 = $ **25 N/m**

[2 marks for correct answer between 24 and 26 N/m, otherwise 1 mark for correct calculation]

2   Work done on spring = energy stored in the spring's elastic potential energy store
         $E = \frac{1}{2}ke^2 = \frac{1}{2} \times 25 \times 0.08^2$ *[1 mark]* = **0.08 J** *[1 mark]*

Page 50 — Moments

1      $M = Fd = 50 \times 0.12$ *[1 mark]* = **6 Nm** *[1 mark]*

2.1   Gear B: clockwise *[1 mark]*
         Gear C: anticlockwise *[1 mark]*

2.2   faster than gear A *[1 mark]*

3   Anticlockwise moment:
         $320 \times 1 = 320$ Nm
         $365 \times (1 + 1) = 730$ Nm
         $320 + 730 = 1050$ Nm *[1 mark]*
         Total anticlockwise moment must equal the total clockwise moment for the seesaw to balance.
         $Fd = 1050$ Nm *[1 mark]*
         $d = 1050 \div 350 = $ **3 m** *[1 mark]*

Pages 51-52 — Fluid Pressure

Warm-up
Liquids and **gases** are both fluids. Fluid pressure is the force exerted **perpendicular** to a surface, per unit **area**. The unit of pressure is **pascals**.

1.1 $p = F \div A$ *[1 mark]*

1.2 $p = 12 \div 0.15$ *[1 mark]* = **80 Pa** *[1 mark]*

2   Pressure increases with depth *[1 mark]* because at a greater depth there are more water molecules above a surface and their weight contributes to the pressure *[1 mark]*. This causes the force pushing the water out of the spouting tank to be larger, so more water leaves the lowest spout in a given time *[1 mark]*.

3   Pressure at a given depth depends on the density of the liquid *[1 mark]*. Sea water has a higher density than fresh water, so the diver experiences a higher pressure *[1 mark]*.

4.1 $A = 0.025 \times 0.025 = 0.000625$ m² *[1 mark]*
         $p = F \div A = 100 \div 0.000625$ *[1 mark]* = **160 000 Pa** *[1 mark]*

4.2 $F = p \times A = 160\,000 \times 0.005$ *[1 mark]* = 800 N
         800×4 *[1 mark]* = **3200 N** *[1 mark]*

5      $p = h\rho g$
         p at X = $0.040 \times 1.0 \times 10^3 \times 9.8 = 392$ Pa *[1 mark]*
         p at base = $0.300 \times 1.0 \times 10^3 \times 9.8 = 2940$ Pa *[1 mark]*
         $2940 - 392 = 2548 = $ **2500 Pa (to 2 s.f.)** *[1 mark]*

Page 53 — Upthrust and Atmospheric Pressure

1   In a liquid, pressure **increases** with depth. This means that the force acting on the bottom of a submerged object is **larger** than the force acting on the top of the object. This leads to a resultant force called **upthrust**.
     [2 marks for all three correct, otherwise 1 mark for one or two correct]

2   When the ball is submerged in the water, upthrust acts upon the ball *[1 mark]*. This is a force that acts in the opposite direction to the ball's weight *[1 mark]* so combining these forces leads to the ball appearing to weigh less *[1 mark]*.

3   The upthrust acting on the necklace is equal to the weight of the water that the necklace displaces *[1 mark]*. Water has a much lower density than silver, so the weight of the displaced water is less than the weight of the necklace *[1 mark]*. This means that the upthrust acting on the necklace is less than its weight, so it sinks *[1 mark]*.

4   How to grade your answer:
         Level 0:   There is no relevant information. *[No marks]*
         Level 1:   There is a brief explanation of the cause of atmospheric pressure. *[1 to 2 marks]*
         Level 2:   There is some explanation of why atmospheric pressure decreases with altitude. *[3 to 4 marks]*
         Level 3:   There is a clear and detailed explanation of why atmospheric pressure decreases with altitude. *[5 to 6 marks]*
     Here are some points your answer may include:
     The atmosphere is a relatively thin layer of air around the earth.
     Atmospheric pressure is caused by air molecules colliding with a surface, which exerts a force on the surface.
     As altitude increases, the atmosphere gets less dense (there are

fewer air molecules in a given volume).
This means that there are fewer air molecules to collide with a surface, so the force and pressure exerted decrease.
The weight of the air molecules above a surface also contributes to atmospheric pressure.
Because there are fewer air molecules as altitude increases, the weight of the air above a surface will also decrease. So the atmospheric pressure decreases too.

Pages 54-55 — Distance, Displacement, Speed and Velocity

Warm-up

Displacement and **velocity** are both **vector** quantities. This means they have both a size and a direction. Speed and **distance** are both **scalar** quantities. They do not depend on direction.

1.1   7 m *[1 mark]*
1.2   12 m *[1 mark]*
1.3

[1 mark for arrow of correct length in the correct direction]
1.4   2 m *[1 mark]*
2   330 m/s *[1 mark]*
3   Any three from: fitness / age / distance travelled / terrain *[3 marks — 1 mark for each correct answer]*
4   No — velocity is speed in a given direction *[1 mark]*. The satellite travels at a constant speed, but is always changing direction so its velocity is always changing *[1 mark]*.
5.1 $s = vt$ *[1 mark]*
5.2   Typical walking speed = 1.5 m/s (accept 1-2 m/s) *[1 mark]*
$t = s \div v = 6000 \div 1.5$ *[1 mark]*
   = **4000 s** (accept 3000-6000 s) *[1 mark]*
5.3   Typical cycling speed = 6 m/s (accept 5-7 m/s) *[1 mark]*
$s = vt$ so $t = s \div v = 6000 \div 6$ *[1 mark]* = 1000 s *[1 mark]*
4000 − 1000 = **3000 s** (accept 1800-5200) *[1 mark]*
5.4 $t = 20 \times 60 = 1200$ s *[1 mark]*
$s = vt$ so $v = s \div t = 9600 \div 1200$ *[1 mark]* = **8 m/s** *[1 mark]*
6   Speed of sound = 331 + (0.6 × −60) = 295 m/s *[1 mark]*
Jet speed = 0.80 × 295 = 236 m/s *[1 mark]*
$s = vt = 236 \times 5.0 \times 10^4$ *[1 mark]* = 11 800 000 m
                            = **11 800 km** *[1 mark]*

Page 56 — Acceleration

Warm-up

A sprinter starting a race — 1.5 m/s²
A falling object — 10 m/s²
A bullet shot from a gun — 2 × 10⁵ m/s²

1   The object is slowing down *[1 mark]*.
2.1 $a = \Delta v \div t$ *[1 mark]*
2.2 $a = \Delta v \div t = 4 \div 1$ *[1 mark]* = **4 m/s²** *[1 mark]*
3   $a = \Delta v \div t$
$t = \Delta v \div a$ *[1 mark]* = 20 ÷ 2.5 *[1 mark]* = **8 s** *[1 mark]*
4   $v^2 − u^2 = 2as$ so
$a = (v^2 − u^2) \div 2s = (18^2 − 32^2) \div (2 \times 365)$ *[1 mark]* = −0.9589...
So deceleration = 1.0 m/s² (to 2 s.f.) *[1 mark]*

Pages 57-59 — Distance-Time and Velocity-Time Graphs

1.1

[3 marks for graph plotted correctly, otherwise 1 mark for three points correct, 1 mark for any suitable straight line]

1.2   360 m (accept between 350 m and 370 m) *[1 mark]*
1.3   210 s (accept between 200 s and 220 s) *[1 mark]*
1.4   E.g. refer to the same point on the boat / make sure that the timings are measured from exactly level with the posts / make sure timings are made close to the posts to avoid parallax / use a stopwatch instead of a watch *[1 mark for any correct answer]*
2.1   12 minutes *[1 mark]*
2.2   Accelerating *[1 mark]*
3.1 $v = \Delta s \div t$ = gradient of line
Speed = (92 − 20) ÷ (6 − 3) = 72 ÷ 3 = **24 m/s**
(accept between 23 m/s and 25 m/s)
[3 marks for correct answer, otherwise 1 mark for realising speed is the gradient of the line, 1 mark for correct calculation]
3.2   Speed = gradient of a tangent to the line
$v = \Delta s \div \Delta t = (16 − 0) \div (3 − 1) = 16 \div 2 = $ **8 m/s**
(accept between 6 m/s and 10 m/s)
[3 marks for correct answer, otherwise 1 mark for a correct tangent to the line, 1 mark for correct calculation]
4.1

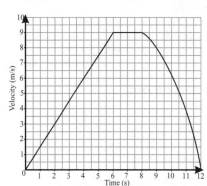

[1 mark for correct shape of graph, 1 mark for graph ending at 0 m/s]
4.2 $a = \Delta v \div t$ = gradient of the line
Acceleration = (9 − 0) ÷ (6 − 0) = **1.5 m/s²**
[2 marks for correct answer, otherwise 1 mark for correct calculation]
4.3 $s = vt$ = area under the line *[1 mark]*
0-6 s: area = ½bh = ½ × 6 × 9 = 27 m *[1 mark]*
6-8 s: area = bh = 2 × 9 = 18 m *[1 mark]*
Total distance in 8 s = 27 + 18 = **45 m** *[1 mark]*
4.4   1 square is worth 0.5 s on the *x*-axis (time)
1 square is worth 0.5 m/s on the *y*-axis (velocity)
[1 mark for both correct]
$s = vt = 0.5 \times 0.5 = 0.25$ m *[1 mark]*
Squares under the line between 8 s and 12 s = 91 *[1 mark]*
91 × 0.25 = 22.75 m *[1 mark]*
Total distance = 45 + 22.75 = 67.75 = **68 m** *[1 mark]*
(accept between 63 and 72 m)

Page 60 — Terminal Velocity

1   The resultant vertical force on an object falling at its terminal velocity is zero.
Terminal velocity is the maximum velocity an object can fall at. *[1 mark for both correct]*
2

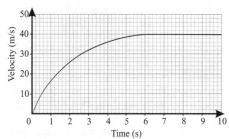

[1 mark for curved shape of graph up to 6 s, 1 mark for straight line at 40 mph after 6 s]
3   As both objects fall, they accelerate due to gravity *[1 mark]*.
As their velocities increase, so does the air resistance acting on them *[1 mark]*. The air resistance acts in the opposite direction to the acceleration, reducing the resultant forces acting on each object. Eventually the resultant forces on the objects are zero and they fall at constant velocities *[1 mark]*. The book

Answers

has a larger surface area than the ball, so experiences more air resistance *[1 mark]*. This means that the resultant force on the book reaches zero sooner, and so it has a lower terminal velocity *[1 mark]*.

Pages 61-62 — Newton's First and Second Laws

1 If the resultant force on a stationary object is zero, the object will remain stationary *[1 mark]*.
2 Newton's Second Law states that the acceleration of an object is **directly** proportional to the **resultant** force acing on the object and **inversely** proportional to the **mass** of the object.
[3 marks for all correct, 2 marks for 2-3 correct, 1 mark for one correct]
3.1 E.g. friction *[1 mark]*, air resistance / drag *[1 mark for either]*
3.2 Resultant force on an object at a constant velocity is zero.
so 5000 = 3850 + second force
Second force = 5000 – 3850 = **1150 N**
[1 mark for correct answer]
4.1 $F = ma$ *[1 mark]*
4.2 $F = 5.0 \times 9.8$ *[1 mark]* = **49 N** *[1 mark]*
5 $a = \Delta v \div t = 24 \div 9.2$ *[1 mark]* = 2.6... m/s² *[1 mark]*
$F = ma = 1450 \times 2.6...$ *[1 mark]* = 3782.6...
= **3800 N (to 2 s.f.)** *[1 mark]*
6 Typical speed of a lorry is 25 m/s
(accept 20-30 m/s) *[1 mark]*
$v^2 – u^2 = 2as$
$a = (v^2 – u^2) \div 2s = (0^2 – 25^2) \div (2 \times 50)$ *[1 mark]*
= –625 ÷ 100 = –6.25 m/s² (accept 4-9 m/s²) *[1 mark]*
$F = ma = 7520 \times –6.25$ *[1 mark]*
= **(–) 47 000 N** (accept 30 100-67 700 N) *[1 mark]*

Page 63 — Inertia and Newton's Third Law

Warm-up
When two objects interact, they exert equal and opposite forces on each other.
1.1 320 N *[1 mark]*
1.2 Normal contact force *[1 mark]*
1.3 640 N *[1 mark]*
Weight is the force exerted by the Earth on the gymnast (because of the gymnast and the Earth interacting). An equal but opposite force acts on the Earth because of the gymnast.
2.1 The tendency to continue in the same state of motion *[1 mark]*
2.2 E.g. how difficult it is to change the velocity of an object / ratio of force over acceleration / $m = F \div a$
[1 mark for any correct definition]

Page 64 — Investigating Motion

1.1 E.g. as force increases, so does acceleration / acceleration is proportional to force
[1 mark for any correct conclusion]
1.2 $F = ma$ *[1 mark]*
1.3 At a force of 4.0 N, the acceleration is 2.25 m/s²
So $m = F \div a$ *[1 mark]* = 4.0 ÷ 2.25 *[1 mark]*
= 1.77... = **1.8 kg** *[1 mark]*
You'll still get the marks if you took readings from a different part of the graph, so long as you get the correct final answer.
2 To test the effect of varying the mass of the trolley, the force on the trolley has to remain constant *[1 mark]*. Adding masses to the trolley increases both the force on and mass of the trolley, so the effect of varying the mass cannot be found *[1 mark]*.

Page 65 — Stopping Distances

1.1 The distance travelled during the driver's reaction time *[1 mark]*
1.2 The distance travelled under the braking force of the vehicle *[1 mark]*
2 Stopping distance = thinking distance + braking distance
12 + 24 = **36 m** *[1 mark]*
3 Work is done by friction between the brakes and the wheels *[1 mark]*. This causes energy to be transferred to the thermal energy stores of the brakes, so they increase in temperature *[1 mark]*.
4 Level 0: There is no relevant information. *[No marks]*
Level 1: There is a brief explanation of why good brakes and tyres are important. *[1 to 2 marks]*

Level 2: There is an explanation of why good brakes and tyres are important with some explanation as to the safety implications of poor brakes or tyres.
[3 to 4 marks]
Level 3: A logical and detailed explanation is given which includes at least 2 examples of explaining the importance of having the tyres and brakes in good condition, at least 2 safety implications and at least 1 effect on stopping distance.
[5 to 6 marks]
Here are some points your answer may include:
A good tread depth on tyres removes water.
This means there is a large amount of grip (friction) between the road and the tyres.
This decreases the braking (and so stopping) distance in wet conditions.
It also means the car will be less likely to skid in wet conditions.
Brakes that are in good condition allow a larger braking force to be applied.
This means that the braking distance of the car is shorter.
Brakes that are in good condition are also less likely to overheat under a large braking force.
So the car is less likely to go out of control or cause a crash.

Pages 66-67 — Reaction Times

1 0.2 - 0.9 s *[1 mark]*
2 Any three from: tiredness / alcohol / drugs / distractions
[3 marks — 1 mark for each correct answer]
3.1 E.g. clicking a mouse when a computer screen changes colour *[1 mark]*
3.2 Student A: (7.0 + 7.1 + 6.9) ÷ 3 = **7.0 cm** *[1 mark]*
Student B: (8.4 + 8.2 + 8.3) ÷ 3 = **8.3 cm** *[1 mark]*
3.3 Student A, because the average distance fallen by the ruler was less for Student A than Student B *[1 mark]*.
3.4 E.g. use the same ruler, always have the same person dropping the ruler. *[2 marks — 1 mark for each correct answer]*
3.5 Their reaction times will get longer *[1 mark]*.
4 Hold a ruler between the open forefinger and thumb of the person being tested *[1 mark]*. Align their finger to the zero line of the ruler, then drop the ruler without warning *[1 mark]* and have the test subject close their thumb and finger to catch the ruler *[1 mark]*. The distance the ruler falls can be read from the ruler *[1 mark]*. The time taken for it to fall can be calculated, as the acceleration (due to gravity) is constant. This is the reaction time of the test subject *[1 mark]*.
5 Level 0: There is no relevant information. *[No marks]*
Level 1: There is a brief explanation of how the man's reaction time may be affected and at least one mention of an implication this has for safety.
[1 to 2 marks]
Level 2: There is an explanation of how the man's reaction time may be affected and the implications this has for safety. *[3 to 4 marks]*
Here are some points your answer may include:
Listening to loud music may mean that the driver is distracted.
This may increase his reaction time.
An increased reaction time means an increased thinking distance.
Driving quicker also increases the distance the car travels during the man's reaction time.
All of these things increase stopping distance, which means the man may not be able to stop in time to avoid hitting a hazard.
He may be unable to see an upcoming hazard because it is dark.
Driving late at night might mean that the man is tired.
He may not be able to hear an upcoming hazard because of the loud music.
This reduces the stopping distance required to avoid hitting a hazard and may lead to the driver having a collision.
6 $v^2 – u^2 = 2as$
$v^2 = 0 + (2 \times 9.8 \times 0.45)$ *[1 mark]* = 8.82
$v = 2.969...$ m/s *[1 mark]*
$a = \Delta v \div t$, so $t = \Delta v \div a = 2.969... \div 9.8$ *[1 mark]*
= 0.303... = **0.30 s (to 2 s.f.)** *[1 mark]*

Answers

Page 68 — More on Stopping Distances

1.1

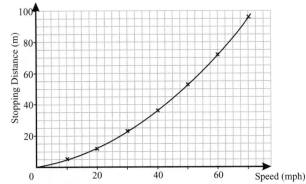

[1 mark for each correctly plotted point, 1 mark for correct line of best fit]

1.2 30 m (accept between 28 m and 32 m) *[1 mark]*

1.3 83 − 30 = **53 m** (accept between 50 m and 56 m)
[2 marks for correct answer, otherwise 1 mark for reading a value correctly from the graph for 65 mph]

2 $s = vt = 18 \times 0.5 = 9$ m *[1 mark]*
So thinking distance is 9 m.
45 − 9 = 36 m *[1 mark]*
So braking distance is 36 m.
If the speed doubles, the thinking distance doubles
$9 \times 2 = 18$ m *[1 mark]*
If the speed doubles, braking distance increases
four-fold (2^2): $36 \times 2^2 = 144$ m *[1 mark]*
Stopping distance = 18 + 144 = **162 m** *[1 mark]*

Page 69 — Momentum

Warm-up
1: Momentum is a property of...
2: ...moving objects.
3: It is a...
4: ...vector quantity and is equal to...
5: ...mass × velocity.

1.1 $p = mv$ *[1 mark]*

1.2 $m = p \div v$ *[1 mark]* = 5500 ÷ 25 *[1 mark]* = **220 kg** *[1 mark]*

2 In Figure 1, the total momentum of the system is equal to the mass of the moving ball multiplied by its velocity *[1 mark]*. As it hits the line of balls, it transfers this momentum to them and comes to a stop. All of this momentum is transferred along the line of balls to the ball at the end of the line, which is why the middle balls don't move *[1 mark]*. This final ball has the same momentum as the first ball, causing it to move with the same velocity (because all of the balls have the same mass) that the moving ball in Figure 1 had *[1 mark]*. In Figure 2, the total momentum of the system is equal to the total momentum in Figure 1 *[1 mark]*.

Page 70 — Changes in Momentum

1 The resultant force acting on the object. *[1 mark]*

2 $F = (m\Delta v) \div \Delta t = 10 \div 0.1 = $ **100 N**
[2 marks for correct answer, otherwise 1 mark for correct calculation]

3 The air bag increases the time taken for the driver to stop *[1 mark]*. This decreases the rate of change of momentum *[1 mark]*. The force exerted on the driver equals the rate of change of momentum so the force on the driver is reduced *[1 mark]*. A lower force on the driver means a reduced risk of injury *[1 mark]*.

4 $p = mv$
Before tackle:
Momentum of first player = 80 × 8.0 = 640 kg m/s
Momentum of second player = 100 × −5.5 = −550 kg m/s
The velocity (and so momentum) is negative for the second player because he is moving in the opposite direction to the first player. For this question, I've taken to the right to be positive.
Total momentum = 640 − 550 = 90 kg m/s *[1 mark]*
After tackle:
Mass = 80 + 100 = 180 kg
Momentum = 180 × v *[1 mark]*

Momentum before = momentum after, so
90 = 180 × v *[1 mark]*
v = 90 ÷ 180 = 0.5 m/s
Magnitude of velocity = 0.5 m/s *[1 mark]*
Direction = to the right *[1 mark]*

Topic 6 — Waves

Page 71 — Transverse and Longitudinal Waves

1.1 Spring A: transverse wave *[1 mark]*
Spring B: longitudinal wave *[1 mark]*

1.2 E.g.

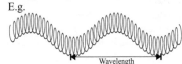

[1 mark for correctly labelled wavelength]

1.3 Amplitude is the maximum displacement of a point on a wave from its undisturbed position *[1 mark]*.

1.4 E.g. ripples on the surface of water / light / any other electromagnetic wave *[1 mark]*

2.1 Horizontal arrow drawn pointing away from the loudspeaker *[1 mark]*

2.2 $T = 1 \div f = 1 \div 200$ *[1 mark]* = **0.005 s** *[1 mark]*

2.3 In longitudinal waves, the oscillations/vibrations are parallel to the wave's direction of energy transfer *[1 mark]*, but in transverse waves, the oscillations/vibrations are perpendicular/at right angles to the wave's direction of energy transfer *[1 mark]*.

Page 72 — Experiments with Waves

1.1 E.g. the student could use a strobe light *[1 mark]*. When the frequency of the strobe light matches that of the wave, the wave fronts will appear stationary (and the student can then measure the stationary wave) *[1 mark]*.

1.2 There are 9 wavelengths in the distance of 18 cm.
Therefore, wavelength = 18 cm ÷ 9 = 2 cm *[1 mark]*
$v = f\lambda = 12 \times 0.02$ *[1 mark]* = **0.24 m/s** *[1 mark]*

2 How to grade your answer:
Level 0: There is no relevant information. *[No marks]*
Level 1: A simple method to find the speed of waves on a string is partly outlined. *[1 to 2 marks]*
Level 2: A method to find the speed of waves on a string is outlined in some detail. *[3 to 4 marks]*
Level 3: A method to find the speed of waves on a string is fully explained in detail. *[5 to 6 marks]*
Here are some points your answer may include:
Connect a string over a pulley to a vibration transducer. Connect a signal generator to the vibration transducer and switch it on.
Adjust the frequency of the signal generator to produce clear waves on the string.
For as many half-wavelengths on the string as you can, measure the distance they cover.
Divide this by the number of half-wavelengths to find the average half-wavelength of the waves on the string.
Double this value to find the wavelength, λ, and note down the frequency of the frequency generator, f.
Use the formula $v = f\lambda$ to calculate the speed of the waves on the string, v.
To get more accurate results the experiment can be repeated for different frequencies and a mean value calculated.

Page 73 — Reflection

Warm-up
wave is reflected — it bounces back off the material
wave is absorbed — it transfers all energy to the material
wave is transmitted — it passes through the material

1

[1 mark for normal lines drawn correctly, 1 mark for the path of the light ray drawn correctly]

2.1 Some of the light is reflected back *[1 mark]* and some of the light is transmitted through the lens *[1 mark]*.

2.2   The damaged lens has a rough surface so it will reflect light in many different directions (diffuse reflection) *[1 mark]*. Therefore, no clearly reflected image will be visible in the damaged lens *[1 mark]*. A clear reflection is seen in the undamaged lens because light is reflected in a single direction by a smooth surface (specular reflection) *[1 mark]*.

Page 74 — Electromagnetic Waves and Refraction

1.1   All waves in the electromagnetic spectrum are **transverse**. *[1 mark]*. All electromagnetic waves travel at the same speed in **a vacuum**. *[1 mark]*

1.2   microwaves *[1 mark]*

1.3   E.g. energy is transferred from the thermal energy store of a toaster's heating element *[1 mark]* by (infrared) radiation to the thermal energy store of bread inside the toaster *[1 mark]*.

2.1

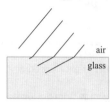

[1 mark for wave fronts bending in the correct direction, 1 mark for wave fronts inside the glass being joined up with those in the air]

2.2

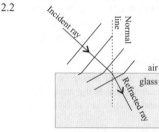

[1 mark for incident ray drawn and labelled correctly, 1 mark for normal line drawn and labelled correctly, 1 mark for refracted ray drawn and labelled correctly.]

Pages 75-76 — Investigating Light

1.1   The angle of incidence and angle of reflection should be equal *[1 mark]*.

1.2   At the mirror: specular reflection *[1 mark]*.
At the card: diffuse reflection *[1 mark]*.

1.3   The rough surface means that the angle of incidence is different for each ray across the width of the beam *[1 mark]*. This means each ray is reflected in a different direction, so the light is scattered *[1 mark]*.

1.4   A ray box was used to provide a thin beam of light *[1 mark]* so that the angles of incidence and reflection could be easily and accurately measured *[1 mark]*. A laser could also have been used to produce similar results *[1 mark]*.

2.1

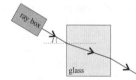

[1 mark for straight line with correct arrow drawn, connecting the two rays at the edge of the block]

2.2   18° *[1 mark for an answer in the range 17° to 19°]*

2.3   The speed of the light ray decreases *[1 mark]* as the angle of refraction, R, is smaller than the angle of incidence, I, i.e. it is bent towards the normal *[1 mark]*.

2.4   The speed of the light ray changes least in water *[1 mark]*. Water has the largest angle of refraction *[1 mark]*, so has bent the light the least (so has slowed the light down the least) *[1 mark]*.

2.5   The material of the container will also refract light *[1 mark]*. The thinner the walls of the container, the less this will affect the results *[1 mark]*.

Page 77 — Radio Waves

Warm-up
True, True, False, True.

1   How to grade your answer:
Level 0:   There is no relevant information. *[No marks]*
Level 1:   A simple method of generating radio waves is described. *[1 to 2 marks]*
Level 2:   A method of generating radio waves and how these waves generate an electrical signal in a distant TV aerial is described. *[3 to 4 marks]*
Here are some points your answer may include:
An alternating current flows in the circuit the transmitter is connected to.
Alternating currents are made up of oscillating charges/electrons.
As the electrons oscillate in the transmitter, they produce oscillating electric and magnetic fields/radio waves.
Radio waves are transmitted to and then absorbed by the distant TV aerial.
The energy carried by the waves is transferred to the electrons in the material of the receiver.
This causes electrons in the receiver aerial to oscillate.
This generates an alternating current/an electrical signal.
This alternating current has the same frequency as the original current used to generate the radio wave.

2   How to grade your answer:
Level 0:   There is no relevant information. *[No marks]*
Level 1:   There is a brief explanation of the differences between radio wave types used for broadcasting *[1 to 2 marks]*
Level 2:   There is some explanation of the differences between radio wave types used for broadcasting, including their different ranges and how this affects which broadcast can be heard. *[3 to 4 marks]*
Level 3:   There is a clear and detailed explanation of the differences between radio wave types used for broadcasting, including their different ranges and how this affects which broadcast can be heard. *[5 to 6 marks]*
Here are some points your answer may include:
FM radio is transmitted using very short wavelength radio waves.
These radio waves can only be received while the receiver is in direct sight of the transmitter.
This is because these wavelengths are easily absorbed by obstacles, e.g. buildings, and cannot diffract.
Therefore, the signal cannot be received in France.
Long-wave radio waves can be transmitted over long distances.
This is because long-wave radio waves diffract around the curved surface of the Earth.
Long-wave radio waves can also diffract around obstacles such as mountains.
Hence the signal can be received in France.

Page 78 — EM Waves and Their Uses

1.1   The microwaves are absorbed by water molecules in the potato *[1 mark]*. This transfers energy to the water molecules, causing the water in the potato to heat up *[1 mark]*. The water molecules transfer the energy they have absorbed to the rest of the molecules in the potato, cooking it *[1 mark]*.

1.2   The glass plate does not absorb any microwaves *[1 mark]* as it does not contain any water molecules, and so it does not heat up *[1 mark]*.

1.3   infrared *[1 mark]*

1.4   Satellites are located above the atmosphere *[1 mark]*. The atmosphere contains water molecules *[1 mark]*. The microwaves used in microwave ovens could not reach satellites as they would be absorbed by water molecules in the atmosphere *[1 mark]*. Different wavelengths which are not absorbed by the atmosphere must be used to communicate with satellites *[1 mark]*.

2   It is dark so there is very little visible light for a normal camera to pick up *[1 mark]*. The person trying to hide is warmer than the surroundings and so emits more infrared radiation *[1 mark]*. This makes the person stand out from the surroundings if observed through infrared radiation *[1 mark]*.

Page 79 — More Uses of EM Waves

Warm-up
UV Rays: A, C, D
Visible Light: B
X-rays: E, F
Gamma Rays: F

1.1 E.g. the patient is injected with a gamma-emitting source *[1 mark]*. Gamma radiation is detected outside of the body, which is used to follow the source's progress around the patient's body *[1 mark]*.

1.2 E.g. they can pass out of the patient's body / they can be detected outside of the patient's body *[1 mark]*.

1.3 X-rays are directed at the patient. The X-rays are absorbed by bones *[1 mark]*, but transmitted by less dense body material, such as flesh *[1 mark]*. A screen behind the patient detects the X-rays and a negative image is formed with brighter areas where fewer X-rays are detected *[1 mark]*.

1.4 E.g. wear lead aprons / stand behind lead screens / leave the room whilst treatment is taking place *[1 mark]*.

Page 80 — Dangers of Electromagnetic Waves

1.1 X-rays and gamma rays transfer so much energy to living cells that they can knock off electrons (ionise atoms) *[1 mark]*. This can cause mutation of genes, leading to cancer *[1 mark]*.

1.2 Any two from: sunburn / premature aging / blindness / (increased risk of) skin cancer *[2 marks]*

2.1 Compare risk of chest scan to risk of head scan,
10 000 ÷ 2500 = 4
Risk is 4 times greater, so dose is 4 times greater *[1 mark]*.
Dose = 2 × 4 = **8 mSv** *[1 mark]*

2.2 How to grade your answer:
Level 0: There is no relevant information. *[No marks]*
Level 1: The risks and benefits are identified but no comparison is made about whether one outweighs the other. *[1 to 2 marks]*
Level 2: There is some discussion about balancing the benefits with the risks. *[3 to 4 marks]*
Level 3: There is a detailed explanation of the benefits and risks, and an informed explanation of why the procedure may go ahead. *[5 to 6 marks]*
Here are some points your answer may include:
The radiation dose is large, so the risk of developing cancer from the procedure is higher than in some other procedures.
However, the procedure might better inform a decision on future treatment.
So future treatment may be more effective.
The benefit of treating the condition needs to be compared with the risk of the procedure (and any subsequent treatment).
An assessment needs to be made about the risk of dying (or poor quality of life) from the underlying condition and the potential benefits for treatment.
Other less risky procedures might lead to similar benefits and these need to be considered.
If the benefits outweigh the risks considerably, then it is worth carrying on with the procedure.

Page 81 — Lenses

1.1

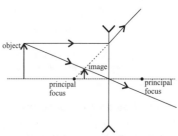

[3 marks — 1 mark for each correct label]
Note: There is another principle focus on the other side of the lens. Labelling either is fine.

1.2 4.5 cm (allow 4.3 — 4.7 cm) *[1 mark]*

1.3 By refracting light *[1 mark]*
Lenses form images by changing the direction of rays of light.

2 E.g.

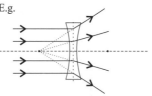

[1 mark for non-central rays diverging once they have passed through the lens, 1 mark for correct construction of refracted rays that are traced back to the principal focus on the correct side]
You could also draw the light rays refracting at each side of the lens — both when they're entering the lens and leaving it. You just need to make sure the light rays leaving the lens trace back to the principal focus.

Page 82 — Images and Ray Diagrams

1.1

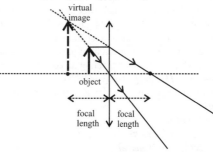

[1 mark for ray through middle of the lens carried on in a straight line, 1 mark for ray parallel to the axis bending at the lens and passing through principal focus, 1 mark for image drawn at the point where the rays meet.]

1.2 It is a real image *[1 mark]*. The light rays come together to form the image *[1 mark]*.
A quick test between virtual and real images — you can project a real image onto a piece of paper, but you can't do the same for a virtual image.

2.1

[1 mark for light ray continued in a straight line through the middle of the lens and traced back, 1 mark for ray parallel to the axis bent towards the principle focus and traced back, 1 mark for image drawn at point the two rays meet, 1 mark for image labelled as a virtual image.]

2.2 Any two from: The new image is a real image while the original is virtual. / The new image is on the opposite side of the lens to the original image. / The new image is the same size as the object while the old image was larger. / The new image is inverted while the old image was the same way up. *[2 marks — 1 mark for each correct answer]*

Page 83 — Concave Lenses and Magnification

1.1 A *[1 mark]*, C *[1 mark]*
Concave lenses always bend light away from the axis — except for rays which pass through the centre of the lens, which pass through unaltered.

1.2

[1 mark for ray drawn from top of object parallel to axis, diverging at the lens so that it is traced back to principal focus, 1 mark for ray drawn from top of object through the centre of the lens, 1 mark for image drawn and labelled at the point where the rays meet.]

2

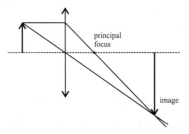

[1 mark for ray through middle of the lens carried on in a straight line, 1 mark for ray parallel to the axis bending at the lens and passing through principal focus.]

Image height is 40 mm (accept between 40 and 45 mm) *[1 mark]*

So magnification = image height ÷ object height

= 40 ÷ 20 *[1 mark]*

= **2** (accept between 2 and 2.5) *[1 mark]*

Pages 84-85 — Visible Light

Warm-up

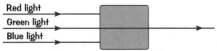

The green light ray should continue in a straight horizontal line on the other side of the block. The red and blue rays should not continue past the block.

1.1 Opaque objects do not transmit light. All light which hits them is either absorbed or reflected *[1 mark]*.

1.2 The white football reflects all wavelengths/frequencies of visible light equally *[1 mark]*, so it appears white. The red football only reflects the wavelengths/frequencies corresponding to red light (it absorbs all other wavelengths/frequencies) *[1 mark]*.

1.3 The red filter is only letting red light pass through it *[1 mark]*. It absorbs all other colours of light from the white ball *[1 mark]*.

1.4 The green filter only lets green light pass through *[1 mark]*. Since the white football is reflecting all colours of light, it appears green *[1 mark]*. The red football looks black because it is only reflecting red light, which is absorbed by the green filter *[1 mark]*.

2.1 opaque *[1 mark]*

A transparent object doesn't absorb visible light.

2.2 The object is blue *[1 mark]*.

The dip corresponds to light of wavelength 470 nm being reflected.

2.3

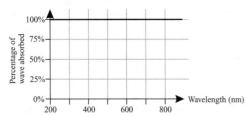

[1 mark for horizontal line at 100% absorption]

2.4

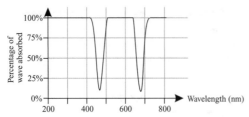

[1 mark for 100% absorption for all wavelengths apart from red and blue, 1 mark for less absorption at 470 nm, 1 mark for less absorption at 680 nm.]

Page 86 — Infrared Radiation and Temperature

1.1 All objects emit and absorb infrared radiation *[1 mark]*.

1.2 The temperature of the object is constant *[1 mark]*.

1.3 The temperature of the object would decrease *[1 mark]*.

2.1 Matte black *[1 mark]*

2.2 Shiny white *[1 mark]*

2.3 E.g. use a radiation detector to measure the emitted radiation

/ use a ruler to make sure he measures the radiation emitted from each side from the same distance *[1 mark for any sensible suggestion]*

Page 87 — Black Body Radiation

1.1 An object that absorbs all of the radiation that hits it *[1 mark]*.

1.2 It has gotten cooler *[1 mark]*.

1.3 The radiation emitted covers a large range of wavelengths *[1 mark]*.

2 How to grade your answer:

Level 0: There is no relevant information. *[No marks]*

Level 1: There is a brief explanation of how the Earth absorbs radiation emitted by the Sun. *[1 to 2 marks]*

Level 2: There is an explanation of how the Earth emits radiation and absorbs radiation emitted by the Sun and how this affects the Earth's temperature at different times of the day. *[3 to 4 marks]*

Level 3: There is a detailed explanation of how the Earth emits radiation and absorbs radiation emitted by the Sun and how the balance between these at different times of the day keeps the Earth's temperature constant. *[5 to 6 marks]*

Here are some points your answer may include:

During the day, the half of the Earth which is facing the Sun is hit by radiation emitted by the Sun.

Some of this radiation is absorbed by the atmosphere and the Earth's surface.

Because of this, the amount of radiation absorbed during the day is greater than the amount that is emitted.

This causes an increase in local temperature.

The half of the Earth which is facing away from the Sun has no radiation from the Sun hitting it — it is night time.

This half of the Earth absorbs very little radiation, but emits radiation at its usual rate.

So at night time radiation is emitted at a much higher rate than it is absorbed.

This causes a decrease in local temperature.

Throughout each full cycle of day and night, one half of the Earth will be increasing in temperature and the other half will be decreasing in temperature.

Overall, these local temperature changes balance out, and so the average temperature of the Earth remains roughly constant.

Page 88 — Sound Waves

1.1 20 Hz to 20 kHz *[1 mark]*.

1.2 The eardrum vibrates when sound waves vibrate the air inside the ear *[1 mark]*, passing these oscillations onto the rest of the ear *[1 mark]*.

3 A child speaks and produces sound wave. The particles in the air vibrate back and forth (creating compressions and rarefactions) as the sound wave travels through the air to the end of the pot *[1 mark]*. When the sound wave hits the pot, the air particles hitting the base of the pot cause it to move back and forth (vibrate) *[1 mark]*. This causes particles in the end of the string tied to the pot to vibrate *[1 mark]*. The particles in the string vibrate and transmit the wave along the string *[1 mark]*. When the vibrations reach the other end of the string, they are transmitted to the base of the second pot. This causes the surrounding air particles to vibrate, generating a sound wave which is heard by the second child *[1 mark]*.

2.2 The frequency stays the same *[1 marks]* and the wavelength increases *[1 marks]*.

Page 89 — Ultrasound

1.1 Vibrations/sound waves with frequencies that are too high for humans to hear *[1 mark]*.

1.2 30 kHz *[1 mark]*, 30 MHz *[1 mark]*

30 Hz is within the human hearing range, so cannot be ultrasound. 30 mHz is outside our hearing range, but its frequency is too low — ultrasound is a high frequency sound wave. Remember that 'm' stands for milli- (× 10⁻³) while 'M' stands for mega- (× 10⁶).

2 Pulses of ultrasound are directed towards the foetus *[1 mark]*. When they reach the boundary between the fluid of the womb and the skin of the foetus, they are partially reflected *[1 mark]*.

The reflections are detected and their timings and distributions are used to produce a video image *[1 mark]*.

3.1   30 ms *[1 mark]*
Measure from the start of the first peak to the start of the second peak.

3.2 $s = vt$
Distance = 1500×0.030 *[1 mark]* = 45 m *[1 mark]*
However, this is twice the distance between the submarine and the ocean floor.
So the distance to the ocean floor = $45 \div 2 =$ **22.5 m** *[1 mark]*

Page 90 — Exploring Structures Using Waves

Warm-up
Is a transverse wave — S-waves
Can pass through a liquid — P-waves
Can pass through a solid — Both

1.1   As there are no S-waves at C, something is stopping them *[1 mark]*. S-waves cannot pass through a liquid so it is likely that part of the interior of the Earth is in a liquid state *[1 mark]*.

1.2   At both points the waves pass between a solid and a liquid medium *[1 mark]*. They travel at different speeds in solids and liquids, so they experience a sudden change in velocity *[1 mark]*.

Topic 7 — Magnetism and Electromagnetism

Pages 91-92 — Permanent and Induced Magnets

Warm-up
non-contact

1.1   A region in which a magnet or magnetic material will experience a force *[1 mark]*.

1.2   Any two of e.g. iron/steel/nickel/cobalt *[2 marks]*

1.3

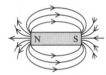

*[2 marks in total — 1 mark for correct shape,
1 mark for arrows pointing from north to south]*

1.4   The correct statements are:
The closer together the magnetic field lines, the stronger the magnetic field *[1 mark]*.
Magnetic field lines point from the north pole to the south pole of a magnet *[1 mark]*.

2.1   The block of cobalt becomes an induced magnet when it is placed in the magnetic field of the bar magnet *[1 mark]*, which causes a force of attraction between the paperclip and the cobalt *[1 mark]*

2.2   When the bar magnet is removed, the cobalt will quickly demagnetise *[1 mark]*, so the paperclip will become unstuck *[1 mark]*.

3.1   How to grade your answer:
Level 0:   There is no relevant information. *[No marks]*
Level 1:   There is a brief description of how the compass should be used. *[1 to 2 marks]*
Level 2:   There is a good description of the method used to determine the magnetic field, including the effect on a compass when placed in a magnetic field. *[3 to 4 marks]*
Here are some points your answer may include:
The needle of a compass points in the direction of the magnetic field it is in.
Put the magnet on a sheet of paper.
Move the compass along the field lines of the horseshoe magnet.
Mark the direction of the compass needle at each point.
Join up the marks to create a diagram of the magnetic field lines.

3.2   E.g. it would point (to geographic) north *[1 mark]* because it is aligning itself with the magnetic field of the Earth *[1 mark]*.

Pages 93-94 — Electromagnetism

1.1

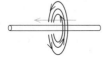

*[2 marks in total — 1 mark for correct shape,
1 mark for correct direction]*
You can work this out using the right-hand thumb rule — point your right thumb in the direction of the current and your curled fingers will show the direction of the field lines. Bingo.

1.2   The direction of the field will also be reversed *[1 mark]*.

1.3   Increase the current *[1 mark]*.

2.1   E.g. a permanent magnet always has a magnetic field, but an electromagnet can be controlled (turned on and off) by an electric current *[1 mark]*.

2.2   E.g. the magnetic field is strong *[1 mark]* and uniform *[1 mark]*.

2.3   If the current is stopped, there will no longer be a magnetic field around the solenoid *[1 mark]*.

3.1   E.g. put a block of iron in the middle of the solenoid *[1 mark]*.

3.2   Repelled *[1 mark]*, because the direction of the current means that the left-hand end of the solenoid acts as a north pole *[1 mark]*, and like poles repel *[1 mark]*.

4   How to grade your answer:
Level 0:   There is no relevant information. *[No marks]*
Level 1:   There is a brief explanation of how the moving hammer strikes the bell. *[1 to 2 marks]*
Level 2:   There is some explanation of how the electromagnet causes the hammer to move. *[3 to 4 marks]*
Level 3:   There is a clear and detailed explanation of how the circuit works. *[5 to 6 marks]*
Here are some points your answer may include:
When the switch is closed, current will flow in the circuit.
The electromagnet will 'switch on' and become magnetised.
This will attract the iron, which will swing the arm on the pivot and cause the hammer to ding the bell.
When the arm pivots, the contacts will move apart from each other, breaking the circuit.
The current will stop flowing, the electromagnet will 'switch off', becoming demagnetised.
The iron will no longer be attracted to the electromagnet, so the arm will swing back to its original position.
This will re-complete the circuit, and the process will start again.
The result is that the bell will continue to ring until the switch is opened again.

Page 95 — The Motor Effect

1.1   It will move towards you, out of the paper *[1 mark]*.
Use Fleming's left-hand rule here. Point your first finger in the direction of the field (i.e. from the north pole to the south pole of the magnets). Point your second finger in the direction of the current (shown in the diagram). Your thumb will then show the direction of motion of the wire.

1.2   E.g. the motor effect *[1 mark]*, caused by the magnetic field of the current-carrying wire interacting with the magnetic field of the permanent magnets (which results in a force) *[1 mark]*.

1.3   The magnetic flux density *[1 mark]*. The current flowing through the wire *[1 mark]*. The length of the wire in the magnetic field *[1 mark]*.

2    $F = BIl$, so $B = F \div Il$ *[1 mark]*
$B = 1.2 \div (0.4 \times 0.75)$ *[1 mark]* = $1.2 \div 0.3 =$ **4 T**
[1 mark for correct value, 1 mark for correct unit]

Page 96 — Electric Motors and Loudspeakers

1   An alternating current is passed through a coil of wire. The coil is surrounded by a **permanent magnet** and attached to the base of a paper cone. When the coil carries a current, it experiences a **force**, so the paper cone moves. This allows variations in **current** to be converted into variations in **pressure** in sound waves. *[3 marks for all correct, otherwise 2 marks for 3 correct, 1 mark for 2 correct]*

2.1   clockwise *[1 mark]*

2.2   E.g. the interacting magnetic fields (of the coil and the magnets) causes a force on each arm of the coil *[1 mark]* in the opposite direction (which causes the coil to rotate) *[1 mark]*.

2.3   E.g. swap the contacts every half turn (e.g. using a split-ring commutator) to reverse the direction of the current *[1 mark]*. This swaps the direction of the forces for each arm and keeps the direction of rotation constant *[1 mark]*.

Page 97 — The Generator Effect

1 Both statements A and B are true *[1 mark]*.

2.1 As the bicycle wheel turns, the generator wheel on the device is turned. This causes the magnet to rotate *[1 mark]*. The coil of wire experiences a change in magnetic field, which induces a potential difference *[1 mark]*. The wires to the lamp form a complete circuit, and so a current is induced *[1 mark]*.

2.2 E.g. By pedalling faster *[1 mark]*.

2.3 The direction that opposes the changing magnetic field caused by the rotating magnet *[1 mark]*.

Page 98 — Generators and Microphones

Warm-up
Alternators use slip rings and brushes and generate ac.
Dynamos use a split-ring commutator and generate dc.

1 The diaphragm is attached to a coil of wire, which is surrounded by (and wrapped around) a permanent magnet *[1 mark]*. When the sound wave hits the diaphragm, the diaphragm moves. This in turn causes the coil of wire to move relative to the magnet *[1 mark]*, which induces (a potential difference, and so) a current (an electrical signal) *[1 mark]*.

2 E.g.

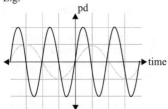

[1 mark for higher peaks, 1 mark for double the initial frequency/twice as many peaks]

Page 99 — Transformers

1 D, A, C, B *[1 mark]*

2.1 $n_p = 12$, $V_p = 240$ V, $V_s = 80$ V, $\frac{V_s}{V_p} = \frac{n_s}{n_p}$

$n_s = \frac{V_s n_p}{V_p}$ *[1 mark]* = (80 × 12) ÷ 240 *[1 mark]* = **4** *[1 mark]*

2.2 step-down *[1 mark]*
There are fewer turns on the secondary coil, and the output pd is less than the input pd.

3.1 $V_p = 12$ V, $n_p = 30$, $n_s = 40$, $\frac{V_s}{V_p} = \frac{n_s}{n_p}$

$V_s = \frac{n_s V_p}{n_p}$ *[1 mark]* = (40 × 12) ÷ 30 *[1 mark]* = **16 V** *[1 mark]*

3.2 $V_s \times I_s = V_p \times I_p$ so $I_s = (V_p \times I_p) ÷ V_s$ *[1 mark]*
I_s = (30 × 20) ÷ 40 *[1 mark]* = **15 A** *[1 mark]*

3.3 E.g. to make transferring electricity more efficient / to reduce energy losses when transferring electricity *[1 mark]*

Topic 8 — Space Physics

Pages 100-101 — The Life Cycle of Stars

1.1 A cloud of dust and gas (in space) *[1 mark]*

1.2 Gravitational force *[1 mark]*

2 In the following order: dust and gas / nebula, protostar, main sequence *[1 mark]*, red super giant *[1 mark]*, supernova *[1 mark]*
Bottom boxes: neutron star (once, in either box) *[1 mark]* black hole (once, in either box) *[1 mark]*.

3.1 As a protostar ages, its **temperature** / **density** and **density** / **temperature** increase. This causes particles to **collide** with each other more often. When the temperature gets hot enough, **hydrogen** nuclei fuse together and create **helium** nuclei. This process is known as nuclear fusion.
[3 marks for all five correct, otherwise 2 marks for three or four correct, 1 mark for one or two correct]

3.2 The outward pressure/expansion due to nuclear fusion *[1 mark]* balances the inwards force due to gravitational attraction *[1 mark]*.

3.3 It keeps the star a steady size *[1 mark]* and keeps the core hot *[1 mark]*.

4 When a star with a mass much greater than the Sun stops being a red supergiant, it expands and contracts several times until it finally explodes in a supernova *[1 mark]*. This leaves behind a very dense core, called a neutron star *[1 mark]* or, if the star was massive enough, a black hole *[1 mark]*.

Pages 102-103 — The Solar System and Orbits

Warm-up
Planet: Neptune, Venus, Earth
Dwarf Planet: Pluto
Natural Satellite: The Moon
Artificial Satellite: Hubble Space Telescope, Communications satellite

1.1 The Sun

1.2 The Milky Way galaxy *[1 mark]*

2.1 The Sun *[1 mark]*
A planet *[1 mark]*

2.2 Gravity *[1 mark]*

2.3 Similarity: e.g. they both have (almost) circular orbits *[1 mark]*. Difference: e.g. moons orbit planets, planets orbit the Sun *[1 mark]*.

3.1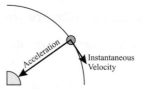

Acceleration: An arrow pointing from the planet to the Sun *[1 mark]*.
Instantaneous Velocity: An arrow at a tangent to the orbit at the planet (as illustrated or in opposite direction) *[1 mark]*.

3.2 How to grade your answer:
Level 0: There is no relevant information. *[No marks]*
Level 1: There is a brief explanation of why centripetal acceleration does not change the speed of the planet. *[1 to 2 marks]*
Level 2: There is some explanation of why the planet's velocity changes but the speed does not. *[3 to 4 marks]*
Level 3: There is a clear and detailed explanation of why the acceleration changes the velocity of the planet, but not its speed. *[5 to 6 marks]*
Here are some points your answer may include:
The acceleration acts along the radius of the orbit, towards the centre.
This means it acts at right angles to the planet's speed (instantaneous velocity).
Acceleration that is perpendicular to the direction of motion does not affect the speed of the motion, it just changes the direction.
Therefore, the speed of the planet is not changed by the acceleration.
Velocity is a vector quantity, with magnitude and direction.
The planet's velocity is constantly changing because its direction is constantly changing.
The acceleration causes the planet to move on a circular path.
Circular motion means that the object experiences changing velocity (i.e. acceleration) but not changing speed.

4 Satellite A has a higher velocity than satellite B *[1 mark]*. The closer the satellite is to the Earth, the stronger the gravitational force on the satellite is *[1 mark]*. This means a larger instantaneous velocity is needed for it to remain in a stable orbit, so satellite A will need to orbit the Earth faster *[1 mark]*.

Pages 104-105 — Red-shift and the Big Bang

1.1 The universe started off hot and dense. *[1 mark]*
The universe is expanding. *[1 mark]*

1.2 E.g. dark matter/dark mass/dark energy *[1 mark]*

2.1 E.g. Galaxies are moving away from each other *[1 mark]*.
More distant galaxies are moving away faster *[1 mark]*.

2.2 They are held together by gravity *[1 mark]*.

2.3 Recent observations of distant supernovae indicate that the speed at which distant galaxies are receding has **increased**.

This suggests that the expansion of the universe is **accelerating**. *[1 mark for each correct]*

3.1 The light's wavelength has increased / is shifted towards the red end of the spectrum *[1 mark]*.

3.2 Tadpole galaxy *[1 mark]*. It is the furthest away *[1 mark]*, so it is travelling away fastest *[1 mark]*, so it has the greatest red-shift.

3.3 It will have increased *[1 mark]*. The universe is expanding, so the galaxy will be further away *[1 mark]* and will be travelling away faster *[1 mark]*. So a greater red-shift will be observed.

3.4 Any value between (but not including) 12 million light years and 37 million light years *[1 mark]*.

Mixed Questions

Pages 106-116 — Mixed Questions

1.1 E.g. a permanent magnet produces its own magnetic field *[1 mark]*. An induced magnet is a material that on becomes magnetic when it is put in a magnetic field *[1 mark]*.

1.2

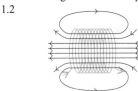

[1 mark for field lines pointing in the correct direction, 1 mark for drawing straight, parallel field lines inside the coil, 1 mark for drawing the field outside the coil]

2.1 E.g. nuclear fallout from nuclear weapons testing / nuclear accidents *[1 mark]*.

2.2 Radioactive decay is where a nucleus releases radiation to become more **stable**. It is a **random** process, which means you **cannot** predict which individual nucleus in a sample will decay next. *[2 marks for all correct, otherwise 1 mark for two correct]*

2.3 E.g. The rate of decay of a source of unstable nuclei/a radioactive source *[1 mark]*.
It is measured in becquerels/Bq *[1 mark]*.

2.4 E.g. the time taken for the activity of a sample to halve *[1 mark]*.

3.1 three-core cable *[1 mark]*

3.2 Live — **brown** — **230** *[1 mark]*
Neutral — blue — **0** *[1 mark]*
Earth — **green and yellow** — 0 *[1 mark]*

3.3 Energy is transferred **electrically** from the mains supply to the **kinetic** energy store of the fan's blades. *[1 mark for each correct answer]*

3.4 Energy transferred = Power × Time = 30 × (30 × 60) *[1 mark]*
= **54 000 J** *[1 mark]*

4.1 C *[1 mark]*

4.2 $V = IR$ *[1 mark]*

4.3 $R = V \div I$ *[1 mark]* = 240 ÷ 1.2 *[1 mark]* = **200 Ω** *[1 mark]*

5.1 sound waves, P-waves *[1 mark for both correct]*

5.2 $T = 1 \div f = 1 \div 40$ *[1 mark]* = 0.025 s
0.025 × 1000 *[1 mark]* = **25 ms** *[1 mark]*

5.3 $v = f\lambda$ *[1 mark]*

5.4 $v = 40 × 0.6$ *[1 mark]* = **24 m/s** *[1 mark]*

6.1

[1 mark for an arrow in the right direction, 1 mark for it being the same length as the driving force arrow]

6.2 $s = vt$ *[1 mark]*

6.3 $s = 5.0 × 30$ *[1 mark]* = **150 m** *[1 mark]*

6.4 $E_k = \frac{1}{2}mv^2 = \frac{1}{2} × 0.50 × 5.0^2$ *[1 mark]* = **6.25 J** *[1 mark]*

6.5 Efficiency = Useful output energy transfer
÷ Total input energy transfer *[1 mark]*

6.6 0.65 = Useful output energy transfer ÷ 1200
Useful output energy transfer = 0.65 × 1200 *[1 mark]*
= **780 J** *[1 mark]*

7.1 The pressure of the water exerts a force on the submerged sides of the cube *[1 mark]*. This leads to a resultant force upwards called upthrust *[1 mark]*, which is equal to the weight of the displaced water *[1 mark]*. The cube is less dense than water, so

it can displace enough water that the upthrust equals its weight (so it floats) *[1 mark]*.

7.2 $\rho = m \div v$ *[1 mark]*

7.3 Volume of water displaced = volume of the cube submerged
Volume = 0.1 × 0.1 × 0.07 = 0.0007 m³ *[1 mark]*
$m = \rho × v$ *[1 mark]* = 1000 × 0.0007 *[1 mark]* = **0.7 kg** *[1 mark]*

8 Calculate the energy to raise the temperature of the water:
$E = mc\Delta\theta$ = 1.2 × 4.2 × 90 *[1 mark]* = 453.6 kJ *[1 mark]*
Energy needed to completely evaporate the water:
$E = mL$ = 1.2 × 2300 *[1 mark]* = 2760 kJ *[1 mark]*
453.6 + 2760 = 3213.6 kJ = **3200 kJ (to 2 s.f.)** *[1 mark]*

9.1 increasing acceleration *[1 mark]*
steady speed *[1 mark]*
constant acceleration *[1 mark]*

9.2 Acceleration = gradient of the graph *[1 mark]*
Acceleration = $\Delta v \div \Delta t$ = (7 − 4) ÷ (7 − 5) *[1 mark]*
= 3 ÷ 2 = **1.5 m/s²** *[1 mark]*

9.3 $F = ma$
So $a = F \div m$ *[1 mark]* = (−)440 ÷ 83 *[1 mark]* = (−)5.30... m/s²
So deceleration = **5.3 m/s²** *[1 mark]*

Remember, force is a vector quantity. It's negative here because it's acting in the opposite direction to the motion of the cyclist. That's what gives you a negative acceleration (deceleration).

9.4 Distance travelled whilst reacting (thinking distance):
Assume a 0.5 s reaction time (accept 0.2-0.9 s) *[1 mark]*
From the graph, the cyclist's speed is 7 m/s, so:
$s = vt$ = 7 × 0.5 = 3.5 m (accept 1.4-6.3 m) *[1 mark]*
Distance travelled whilst braking (braking distance):
$v^2 − u^2 = 2as$
u = 7 m/s, v = 0, a = −5.3 m/s
$s = (v^2 − u^2) \div 2a$ = $(0^2 − 7^2) \div (2 × −5.3)$ *[1 mark]*
= −49 ÷ −10.6 = 4.62... m *[1 mark]*
Stopping distance = thinking distance + braking distance
= 3.5 + 4.62... = 8.12... m = 8.1 m
(accept 6.0-11.0 m)
Stopping distance is less than 12 m, so the cyclist won't hit the car *[1 mark]*.

10.1 $p = F \div A$ *[1 mark]*

10.2 $F = p × A$ *[1 mark]* = 1200 × 0.005 *[1 mark]* = **6 N** *[1 mark]*

10.3 $p = h\rho g$ so
$\rho = p \div hg$ *[1 mark]* = 2850 ÷ (0.15 × 10) *[1 mark]*
= **1900 kg/m³** *[1 mark]*

10.4 How to grade your answer:
Level 0: There is no relevant information. *[No marks]*
Level 1: There is a brief explanation of how increased density means an increase in the number of collisions in a given time, which leads to an increase in pressure. *[1 to 2 marks]*
Level 2: There is a clear explanation of how increased density means an increase in the number of collisions in a given time and an increase in the weight above a surface at a given depth. There is a brief description of how both of these cause an increase in pressure. *[3 to 4 marks]*
Here are some points your answer may include:
The new liquid is denser than water, so there are more particles in a given volume for the new liquid.
This means there are more collisions for a given area in a given time.
This means that there is a higher pressure for a surface in the new liquid.
There are also more particles above a surface at a given depth in the new liquid.
This means the weight of the particles above a given depth is larger for the new liquid than for water.
So the pressure is higher.

11.1 E.g.

[1 mark for wave fronts correctly changing direction, 1 mark for wave fronts being spaced further apart]

Answers

11.2 How to grade your answer:

Level 0: There is no relevant information. *[No marks]*

Level 1: There is a brief description of how the speed of different parts of the wave front change between air and diamond. *[1 to 2 marks]*

Level 2: There is a good description of how different parts of a wave front travel at different speeds when crossing a boundary. There is some description of how this results in refraction. *[3 to 4 marks]*

Level 3: There is a detailed explanation of how the difference in speed for different parts of a wave front results in a difference in distance travelled. There is a clear description of how this results in refraction when crossing a boundary at an angle. *[5 to 6 marks]*

Here are some points your answer may include:

Light travels faster in air than it does in diamond.

When the light ray crosses the boundary between diamond and air at an angle, it means different parts of the wave front cross the boundary at different times.

The parts of the wave front that have crossed the boundary travel faster than the rest of the wave front that is still travelling through the diamond.

Distance = speed ÷ time.

So in the time it takes the entire wave front to cross over the boundary, the parts of the wave front that have spent more of that time travelling through air have travelled further.

This difference in distance travelled between points along the wave front causes the ray to bend (refract) away from the normal.

12.1 E.g.

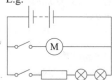

[2 marks for all circuit symbols correctly drawn, otherwise 1 mark for 4 symbols correctly drawn. 1 mark for filament lamps and resistor in series with each other, 1 mark for motor in parallel with other components, 1 mark for correct placement of switches]

12.2 $E = QV$ and $Q = It$ so $E = VIt$ *[1 mark]*

$E = 6.0 \times 70.0 \times 10^{-3} \times (15 \times 60)$ *[1 mark]* = 378 J

$\Delta E = mc\Delta\theta = 0.0250 \times 120 \times 6$ *[1 mark]* = 18 J

$378 - 18$ *[1 mark]* = **360 J** *[1 mark]*

12.3 E.g. he could lubricate the parts within the motor *[1 mark]*. This would reduce friction and the amount of energy being wasted/dissipated to the thermal energy store of the motor *[1 mark]*.

13.1 $V_p \div n_p = V_s \div n_s$

So $V_s = (25\,000 \div 1400) \times 21\,000$ *[1 mark]* = 375 000 V *[1 mark]*

(For a 100% efficient transformer, power in = power out, so:)

$V_p I_p = V_s I_s$

$I_s = (25\,000 \times 4100) \div 375\,000$ *[1 mark]*

= 273.3... = **270 A (to 2 s.f.)** *[1 mark]*

13.2 Power transferred out of the generator = power transferred to the step-up transformer

Power output of generator = VI = 25 000 × 4100

= 1.025×10^8 W *[1 mark]*

Power input of generator

$P = E \div t = (34.92 \times 10^9) \div 60$ *[1 mark]* = 5.82×10^8 W *[1 mark]*

Efficiency = useful power output ÷ total power input

= $1.025 \times 10^8 \div 5.82 \times 10^8$ *[1 mark]* = 0.1761...

= **18% (to 2 s.f.)** *[1 mark]*

13.3 In the national grid, energy is transferred electrically to the thermal energy stores of the wires *[1 mark]* (this is an unwanted energy transfer). This transfer occurs because a moving charge does work against resistance *[1 mark]*, and work causes a transfer of energy *[1 mark]*. Current is the rate of flow of charge *[1 mark]*, so reducing the current reduces the work done and the energy transferred to thermal energy stores *[1 mark]*.

14.1 How to grade your answer:

Level 0: There is no relevant information. *[No marks]*

Level 1: There is a brief description of how a fission reaction occurs, limited to the splitting of a large unstable nuclei into two smaller nuclei. *[1 to 2 marks]*

Level 2: There is a clear description of how a forced nuclear fission reaction occurs. There may be some mention of control rods. *[3 to 4 marks]*

Level 3: There is a clear and detailed description of how a forced nuclear fission reaction occurs. There is a mention of the energies of the fission products and a clear description of how control rods are used to control the energy produced by a fission reactor. *[5 to 6 marks]*

Here are some points your answer may include:

A neutron is absorbed by a radioactive isotope.

This causes it to become more unstable, so it decays.

It splits into two new, lighter elements that are roughly equal in size.

It also releases two or three neutrons.

All of these products have energy in their kinetic energy stores.

Any excess energy is transferred away by gamma rays.

This energy is used to generate electricity.

The neutrons released by an isotope decaying go on to be absorbed and cause more decays / create a chain reaction.

The control rods are lowered into the reactor to absorb neutrons, which reduces the amount of decaying nuclei / which reduces the rate of fission.

This slows down the rate that energy is released.

This reduces the output power (rate of energy transfer) of the power plant.

14.2 How to grade your answer:

Level 0: There is no relevant information. *[No marks]*

Level 1: There is a brief explanation of the safety implications of storing nuclear waste. *[1 to 2 marks]*

Level 2: There is some explanation of the safety implications of storing nuclear waste with some reference being made to half-life. *[3 to 4 marks]*

Level 3: There is a clear and detailed explanation of the safety implications caused by storing nuclear waste and of the precautions needed, including a reference to the penetrating and ionising power of the radiation produced and the half-life of the waste. *[5 to 6 marks]*

Here are some points your answer may include:

The caesium has a half-life of 30 years, so it will take 30 years for the activity of the waste to halve.

This means that the surrounding area will be exposed to radiation for a long time.

The gamma rays released by the waste can travel a large distance before ionising an atom.

This means that a large area surrounding the nuclear waste will be irradiated.

Exposure to nuclear radiation is harmful to humans.

It can kill cells or cause gene mutations which can lead to cancer.

So nuclear waste should be stored far away from humans and other living creatures.

Shielding should also be put around the storage sites of nuclear waste to reduce irradiation.

ISBN 978 1 78294 489 8

9 781782 944898

PAQA41 £2.00
(Retail Price)